AT HOME IN

PROVENCE

RECIPES AND STORIES FROM LIFE IN THE SOUTH OF FRANCE

AT HOME IN
PROVENCE

RECIPES AND STORIES FROM LIFE IN THE SOUTH OF FRANCE

STYLING BY
FRANKIE UNSWORTH

JEANY CRONK
OF MAISON MIRABEAU

Quadrille

PROVENCE, MY HOME...

I spend so much time talking about Provence, trying to describe what makes it so special and captivating, but my words always seem inadequate. The idea most people have of Provence – as France's quintessential holiday spot, full of lavender fields and orderly vineyards – barely captures its essence. That's why I have dreamed of writing this book for so long. While living here with my family over the last decade and a half, this place has revealed itself to be a feast for the eyes and senses, and I can't wait to share this journey with you.

Provence and the Côte d'Azur have a rich history, from Avignon being a temporary papal residence in the 14th century to becoming the destination of choice for wealthy Americans and Russians, spending their winter holidays in style on the Riviera at the turn of the 20th century. The influence of the Greeks and Romans shows up in architecture, culture and cuisine; examples range from the thermal baths of Aix-en-Provence to the remnants of a Roman city in the Cimiez neighbourhood in Nice that once was the size of Pompeii. Crucially for Provence, the Greeks introduced vineyards to the region, as well as the extensive use of olives and their golden oil to their local dishes.

Over the centuries, many writers and painters have come here for inspiration, and our region is still a vibrant hub of creativity today. When travelling here, you'll take turns marvelling at this artistic diversity and the region's magnetic natural beauty. On the way, you'll encounter villages perched on hillsides and navigate charming narrow streets before arriving at glamorous beachside locations overlooking the glittering Mediterranean Sea. There are towns with grand, tree-lined avenues and golden-hued streetscapes, hundreds of stone-carved fountains in shaded squares and the chance to experience a charming moment almost everywhere you go.

The four sections in this book take you on a tour of our villages and vineyards, coastal and city life. Each chapter tells the story of some of the most beautiful spots, with easy-to-follow recipes inspired by typical local produce.

By now, you may be asking yourself what brought me here. Why did my family risk our well-established life in suburban South West London to try to find a new beginning? The reasons are manyfold, but the most important one was that my husband Stephen and I felt that our destiny lay here, in the most southern tip of France. Both of us had ties to the area — my family had a small house near the coast during my childhood and Stephen passed a few happy holidays here, feet in the sand, glass of rosé in hand — but our desire to move here was underpinned by Stephen's wish to return to his first career — his real passion — the world of wine. As well as marketing wine, we wanted to make it ourselves, and create our own distinctive brand.

Provence appealed to us not only because it was already famous for its pale and delicate rosés, but also because its wines were linked

inextricably to our happiest moments. We clinked glasses with a Provence pink during our first date at a French restaurant. Once we started to live together in London, rosé was our staple for dinner on a warm evening *à deux* or if we were headed to the park with a picnic rug and a basket. It paired so nicely with so many foods and both of us loved eating and drinking in the effortless way we had seen during our stays in France.

Relocating here was a circuitous route and took many years of discussion, both between the two of us and our startled families. We also sought out and talked to others who had been through similar adventures. Once we had decided that we were going to leave, not everything went according to plan. We were almost blown off course by the world economic crisis and then by our initial fruitless search to find a

house near a school for our family of five. Eventually, on the advice of a newfound friend, we abandoned our plans to move to the pretty city of Aix-en-Provence, which had initially seemed so perfect for a soft landing. Instead, we followed our acquaintance to a tiny village in the upper Var that I'd never even heard of, called Cotignac, which would immerse us completely into rural French life.

I know I'm lucky to call this beautiful corner of the world my home and I have loved raising my three children here, inside a strong community and with so many experiences that I treasure. Our passion for the unique rosé wines of Provence soon became our profession, and we've had a lively business journey building Maison Mirabeau over the last decade. I've lived through the most beautiful and inspiring moments, but also through painfully tough ones. But these various

'When you watch your kids running around the table laughing and your friends enjoying themselves – those are the episodes in which life is without etiquette and effort.'

waypoints on our journey have made me who I am today and encouraged me to grow personally in a way I would not have been able to on another path. This brings me to the core of this book: the food and *art de vivre*, or the art of living, we so love in Provence. I had been a keen home cook all my life, but coming here was like a little culinary awakening. Provence is the kitchen garden of France, producing some of its tastiest fruit and vegetables, served up on restaurant tables all over the country. There are the delicious melons, peaches and figs you can buy at almost any street corner, but you can also find precious truffles and saffron when they're in season. Rare flowers, for some of the world's most famous perfumes, are grown here too, distilled to be blended by the celebrated 'noses' in the perfume capital of Grasse.

And it's not just the produce that delivers such an amazing sensory experience, it's also how we choose to eat it. I've observed numerous people, many of them regulars in the world's best restaurants, genuinely enjoying themselves while tucking into a fougasse dipped in fresh local olive oil, washed down with a cool glass of rosé de Provence. The beauty of good, seasonal ingredients is that they transform dishes so that they feed us with joy.

I also believe that, as humans, we're meant to share our food, and here in Provence these easy moments together happen often. We're into improvising, handing spoons to one another to taste, eating with our fingers, laughing and sitting back at the end of a meal full of happiness, everyone longing for a *sieste* under an olive tree. What I'm so excited to share with you here, through the many tasty recipes and styling ideas, is how to create these precious moments for yourself, as often as you can. Moments that you wish could last forever, when time is suspended

as you squint into the golden sun rays while the wind tousles your hair. When you watch your kids running around the table laughing and your friends enjoying themselves – those are the episodes in which life is without etiquette and effort.

Over the years in Cotignac and beyond, we've been blessed to meet so many interesting people who have come here to live or visit from all over the world, with their own ideas and life projects. None has impacted me more so than my stylist and co-author Frankie, who has helped me birth this book, which had previously been only a dream. She'll no doubt enrich the lives of so many here in

the village, having settled with her own little family to immerse herself fully into local life, just like I did all those years ago. Most of all, I am full of joy that you're picking up this book and I know you'll create special moments aplenty in your own home, when making some of these flavourful dishes. After all, with good food, friends and a nice glass of wine, *la vie est belle* (life is beautiful)!

Jeany
x

THE VILLAGE

LE VILLAGE

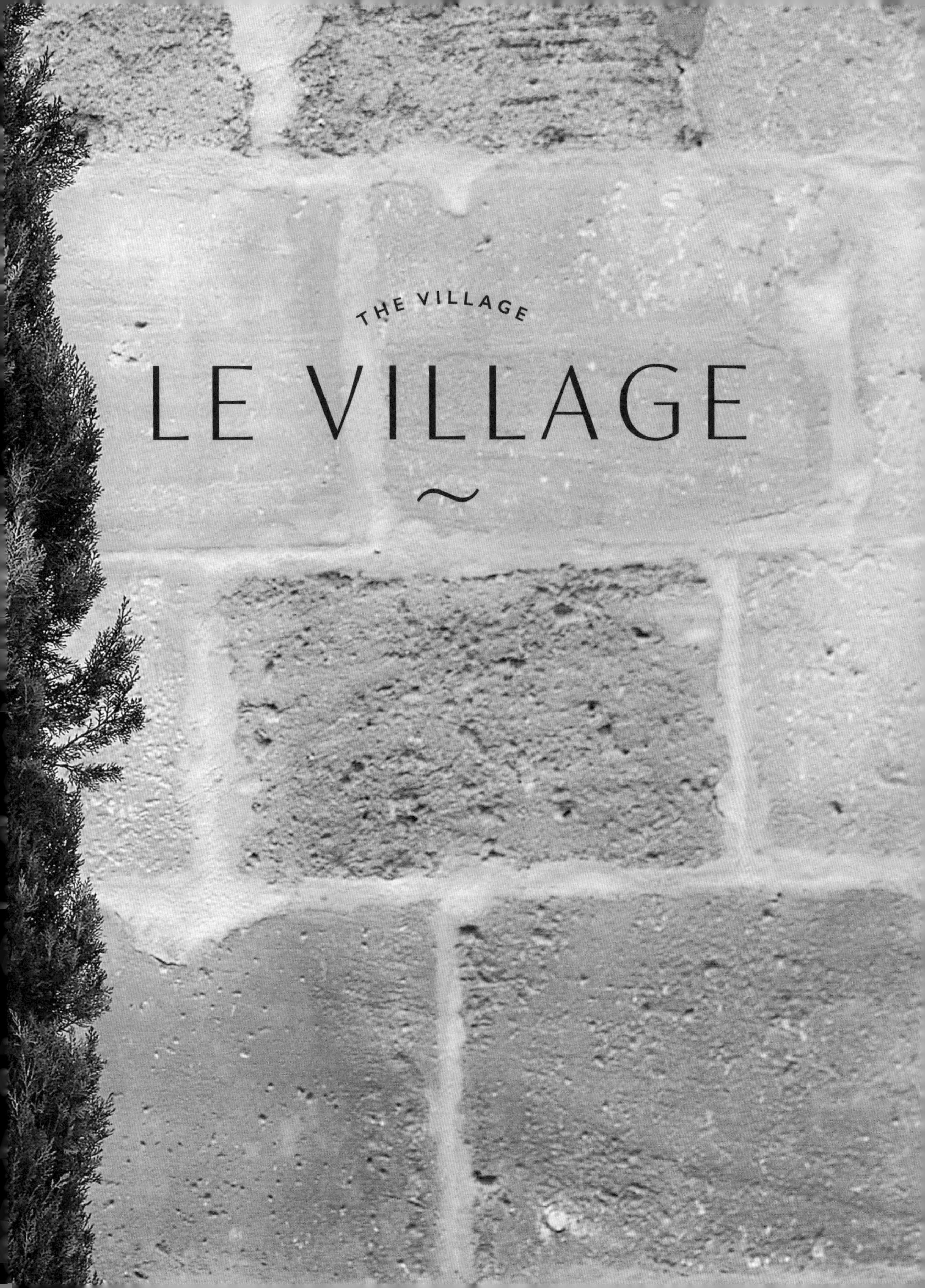

~

A FAMILY IN PROVENCE

After our unsuccessful property search near Aix-en-Provence, Cotignac became our rather unexpected home. When people ask us how we chose this cute little village, I always respond that somehow it chose us. And, given how many people we have met over the years in far-flung places who ended up having a link to Cotignac, and the many interesting characters that have made it their home, we know there is a special kind of magic to the village.

Cotignac is located in the upper Var department, near the Verdon natural park and a good thirty minutes of bendy roads from the motorway, that will test your tyres and power steering. It's a unique example of the perched villages that are so typical of this area, as it is at the foot of an impressive limestone cliff face, carved out by a waterfall over the last two million years. The houses merge into the rocks, and some are chiselled into the actual stone, giving it a slightly otherworldly feel. Below, rows of houses have bright, colourful render, with contrasting painted wooden shutters. Cotignac is arranged over two cobblestone squares, separated by a narrow road, ironically called 'La Grande Rue', full of galleries, gift shops and pottery studios.

There are plenty of restaurants on the main square that serve typical Provençal cuisine, where it's blissful to sit in the shade of the giant trees and watch the world go by. In summer, the village is busy with families, the kids eating ice creams and their parents tucking into a chilled rosé and some confit olives. In winter, it's much quieter and we have the place back to ourselves, with fewer visitors. It's the time of the local hunters and their dogs hanging out in the bars after the *chasse* (hunt), artists and artisans drinking coffee together and everyone catching up on village gossip.

Yet, in spite of its obvious charm, the beginning here was not quite as easy as I'd hoped. The village school that Stephen had been to visit in a suit and tie in 36°C (97°F) heat, much to the amusement of the other parents, was a tough start for our two older kids. Not only did they not speak much French, but they knew no one and had no friends. Our middle son, Felix, spent every morning clinging to one of us, begging us to take him home again. Our eldest, Josie, settled in more easily, but didn't really understand her lessons at school and found it tough to read and write in French. But after a few months, the mornings got easier, and some new friends began to appear in their lives and our own. We all felt relieved that we'd probably been through the worst of it and that, finally, happier days were here!

Soon another creature made his arrival in our family known. To give the kids as much distraction as possible, we had succumbed to their demands for a family dog. After a short search, we lost our heart to a spotty Jack Russell puppy, took him home and named him Oscar. He knitted us together and helped us cope with the many things our new beginning in France threw at us, in a way only a permanently enthusiastic dog can.

Despite the initial anguish, one undeniable perk of French school was the fabulously gourmet school menu! Said menu was pinned up on a message board outside the gate and changed weekly. The school had a kind-hearted, but occasionally fearsome, cook called Maryse, who made things from scratch and insisted the kids try everything. Since nothing works like peer pressure, my beige-food-loving child Felix started eating the many foods I had unsuccessfully attempted to get him to consume for many years. And we all know that when we eat well, life's problems become so much more manageable.

The little ones feasted on tuna fillet with caper sauce, pumpkin soup, homemade burgers, mussels (when in season), cheese platters, escalope and daube, the traditional Provençal stew – and all of it for less than the cost of a sandwich elsewhere! I think most of us parents would have made a beeline to eat there too, given half the chance.

SETTLING DOWN

One thing neither Stephen nor I had bargained for was the time it would take us to find a house of our own in Cotignac. These little villages in the back country of the Var were once upon a time the most rural part of Provence. By the coast or further west, around Aix-en-Provence and towards Avignon, where all the glamorous goings-on took place, the housing stock is much more plentiful. So, while I fell in love with the rolling hills and beautiful woodlands of this area, once here, we found very few family houses were for sale and even less building land. Locals can make a nice income renting properties during the summer season, so there is no immediate pressure to sell if you inherit or move away.

After many viewings, we came to the conclusion that we would like to build a house of our own. That's quite an undertaking in Provence, because good builders and tradesmen are rare and, even when you find them, a project here requires patience. Not much is rushed and many builders juggle multiple jobs, so waiting is part of the process. When I finally found an available plot, I pounced. There was still a lot of work ahead, but this one was surrounded by an old stone wall and the land was terraced over several levels, with some established oak and olive trees and the stunning view I had been hoping for.

I had long decided that I wanted to build a *bastide Provençale*. A *bastide* is the equivalent of a country house, a symmetrical rectangular building made from plaster and stonework, with a big arched door dominating its centre, often leading down to a garden over several levels. The roofs are tiled with the classic terracotta *tuile canal*. They are neatly stacked on top of each other to provide a beautiful architectural detail that glows in the sunshine, and is typical of the south of France. I was determined to construct a modern French *bastide*, but wanted to include details that would ensure it looked like it belonged here from the word go. A stonemason friend made my windowsills by hand, each one chiselled to look old and uneven, and he also built me a beautiful fountain by the side of the terrace so we could listen to the calming sound of running water while we ate. After much experimentation, I found the perfect render that would look nuanced and authentic.

Handmade ironmongery is an important visual feature for Provençal houses, and balustrades and pergolas add a nice contrast of materials, as well as being practical. It's also typical to find cast-iron tables, with caustic or glazed tiles inset as a tabletop. This is a lovely way to have a table that is weatherproof, but with an interesting design or a splash of colour. Pergolas are usually covered with reeds, bringing a soft, dappled light to the much-needed shade.

While I was looking for a fairly modern interior design for my house, with plenty of light and larger spaces, I also wanted to find the right balance and include objects with a nod to the past. A great way to do this is to use crockery and jars, often part-glazed and made from the local *terre cuite* (terracotta). Down the road, in the village of Salernes, terracotta pots and crockery are still made by hand, but you can also find plenty of vintage items at flea markets and antique markets called *brocantes*. Often, these pre-loved pieces bear the scratches of food being spooned out of them over many years, as well as small cracks, weathered patina or imperfect finishes. I love them even more for this visible history. Imperfection can be what adds interest and makes a good counterpoint to more modern, clean lines. Linen, flax and cotton textiles work best in these situations and have the right texture to harmonise with our modern Provençal interiors. Natural stone colours and off-whites bring visual freshness and make a great backdrop for accents of amber, rust, muted pink or warm blues. The general rule is to keep everything light and unfussy and to be inspired by the colours of the landscape.

THE PROVENÇAL MARKET

Here, the highlight of the week is our village market, taking place every Tuesday. Pretty much every village in Provence has a weekly market, some have two, and the bigger towns have one every day. It starts early, around 7.30 a.m., and in summer it gets very busy with people driving in from all over the immediate region. Our market is well known for its plentiful vegetable stands, but it also has stallholders with a big selection of olive products and condiments, as well as a few selling pretty hats, baskets and other artisanal pieces.

The market is a great place to catch up with gossip and have a break with a good coffee and a croissant. For many locals, it's also an essential service, especially for older folk, who may find it hard to drive to the bigger shops and for whom it's a nice social moment at the heart of the village. In winter, the markets become much smaller, but you may find delicacies such as truffles for sale alongside your winter vegetables.

Of course, it takes a while, and some trial and error, to find your favourite stall owners for fruit, vegetables, olives and cheeses. For a nice lunch or aperitif snacks, I pick up homemade green and black olive tapenades, nuts, garlic in brine and sundried tomatoes. As with most markets, local farmers bring their freshly harvested produce. We have organic farmers, who come in from the nearby village of Correns. The vegetables are home-grown on their smallholdings, often sold with bits of soil still on them, and are delicious in the way only something so freshly picked can be. It's great to buy from these local producers through the seasons, from autumnal (fall) pumpkins to winter's rainbow chard and kohlrabi, followed by spring's strawberries and melons and finally summer's ripe tomatoes, peaches and apricots. Given that every market visit is so inspiring, I rarely plan any meals ahead and cook with what I find on the day, reinventing and adjusting recipes to the fresh produce.

EATING AT HOME

The joys of great market finds mean you can create a slap-up lunch for your family or friends with ease. Our lunches are always very relaxed and heavy on vegetables and salads, condiments, fresh bread and simple grilled meat or fish. It's the hottest time of the day, so we like to keep it low-effort and use sharing platters. That way, everyone can eat exactly how much they fancy and we don't have to carry much back and forth once the table is laid. Desserts should be delicious and light, like the gorgeous Lemon Madeleines with white chocolate dip (see page 51).

A tablecloth is optional, and we love to use simple white stoneware plates set on linen or rattan placemats to let the food shine. You can then have more fun with platters and serving dishes, using something striking and colourful, if the rest of the tablescape is more neutral. I always add natural touches to my tables by using vases of different shapes and sizes, with a mix of shop-sourced and foraged plants for a natural feel.

Cutting flowers to different lengths and arranging them freely also feels less 'done'. Flowers or herbs in pots are also fun to use and are a sustainable way to decorate as they can be reused and planted. Thyme, rosemary or verbena work well in a beautiful pot on a rustic table, and you can encourage your guests to add more culinary herbs to their dishes as you eat – it's a scented pleasure to tear up herbs at the table. I sometimes like to add a sprig of rosemary, an olive branch or a small fig leaf as an extra on the napkins or above each plate. On a hot day, include some flavoured water in glass jugs – it looks beautiful and complements the food. I tend to use typical Provençal herbs, like rosemary or verbena, which keep their colour and shape. Use simple linen napkins that provide a nice accent of colour.

THE IMPORTANCE OF QUALITY

One of the elements for which there is not much of a shortcut is food quality. It's easier said than done, especially with our busy lives, but it is important to try to choose good, seasonal ingredients, including olive oil, salt and spices. There are many vegetarian dishes in this book, as well as simpler cuts of meat and fish, which only need a drizzle of good oil and a pinch of crystal salt (*fleur de sel*) to elevate them. Finding a good source for vegetables is key, as these ingredients will take pride of place on your table – if possible, buy from a market stall or dedicated fruit and vegetable shop. We cook them in a way that preserves their natural taste, dressing them with oils, citrus and herbs to bring out their flavour in the most stunning way.

PROVENÇAL INGREDIENTS AND CUISINE

Provençal cuisine, above all else, is based on good, simple ingredients. The fundamental notion of a dish à *la Provençal* usually means that you'll find it cooked with olives, tomatoes and plenty of aromatic herbs, alongside good olive oil. The so-called *garrigue* herbs – a reference to the local shrubland – grow wild everywhere and provide our dishes with the many typical herbaceous notes: oregano, thyme, rosemary, bay, marjoram or *sariette* (winter savoury). Basil also features frequently, and is the basis for our pesto condiment, called *pistou*, which is often used in soups. Other spices we use frequently are the local chilli spice (*piment d'Espellette*) and fragrant pink pepper (*baies roses*).

Vegetables that thrive in our Mediterranean climate are prominent in our cuisine and there are often several colours or varieties on offer. Tomatoes come in all shapes and sizes, from the big beef tomatoes (*coeur de boeuf*), green zebras and yellow pineapple (*ananas*) varieties to all sorts of tasty bush tomatoes. Courgettes (zucchini) can be yellow as well as pale or dark green, and aubergines (eggplants) sometimes come in a pretty striped variety. Courgette flowers (*fleurs de courgette*) are available most of late spring and early summer and are a particular speciality in Provençal cuisine (see our recipe on page 59), sometimes filled with goat's or sheep's cheese, or deep-fried in a tempura batter (*beignets*).

In summer, you'll find plenty of seafood on the menu, with the eponymous *bouillabaise* fish soup from Marseille being the undisputed highlight of a great seafood feast. It's fairly tricky to make, so we have included a simplified version here on page 164. Delicate red mullet (*rouget*), meaty sea bream (*dorade*), sweet sea bass (*loup de mer*) or fresh anchovies are all offered here abundantly in shops and seafood markets. Filleted or cooked whole, they are often simply served with a glug of good olive oil, crystal salt, lemon and thyme, or with tomatoes, making the most of their freshness and market vegetables.

In the colder seasons, we will tuck into a hearty red wine beef stew (*daube*) with plenty of garlic, orange zest and black olives to flavour the slow-cooked meat. It's served with starchy potatoes, pasta or a creamy polenta, which is the nicest combination I find. Lamb tends to be slow-roasted on the bone, usually shoulder or leg (*épaule/gigot*), with plenty of garlic and Provençal herbs and olive oil. The best lamb comes from Sisteron, a town just north of here, but often called the gateway to Provence. Classic stuffed vegetables (*légumes farcis*), including tomatoes, courgettes and bell peppers,

with a garlic-heavy mix of pork and beef (*la farce),* are delicious whatever the season. On page 128 we show you a delicious slow-cooked chicken (*coq au vin*), but this time braised in rosé instead of white wine. Preserved meats (*charcuterie*), dried sausage (*saucisson*) and pâtés, are a big part of social eating here, either as a meal in itself with bread, olives and other condiments, or as an aperitif starter before the main course.

Cheeses are, of course, also enjoyed here in Provence. We major on soft cheeses, often sheep and goat, as cows don't thrive in our climate. The goat's cheeses (*chèvre*) in particular can be very local and are often presented wrapped in leaves or rolled in charcoal, herbs, or colourful pepper. We tend to serve them with quince, fig or persimmon chutneys (Page 135 and 145) and it's traditional to eat a green leaf salad with the cheese course, which I have adopted wholeheartedly.

As in the rest of France, baked goods are of high importance in Provence and you will find some typical local iterations of bread and patisseries in the many bakeries (*les boulangeries*). On the savoury front, a local focaccia bread called *fougasse* (page 111) is delicious and can be found in plenty of flavours and, of course, there is the classic onion and anchovy pizza, *la pissaladiere*. Many bakeries also sell a selection of sourdough breads, called *pain au levain*. Local sweet specialities are the eponymous brioche cake of Saint Tropez, *la Tropézienne*, or a delicious almond and vanilla twisted puff pastry treat, *le sacristain*, and the melon and almond sweets from Aix-en-Provence, *les calissons*.

PEA, CUCUMBER AND MINT CHILLED SOUP

SERVES 4–6

olive oil, for cooking
1 large, sweet onion,
   roughly chopped
1 garlic clove, roughly chopped
300 g (10½ oz/2 cups)
   fresh or frozen peas
180 ml (6 fl oz/scant ¾ cup)
   vegetable stock
handful of ice cubes
2 cucumbers, halved, deseeded
   and roughly chopped
200 ml (7 fl oz/scant 1 cup)
   crème fraîche
fleur de sel and freshly ground
   black pepper
mint leaves, roughly chopped,
   to serve

I am a huge fan of a refreshing, cool soup in summer, and there's nothing that does it as well as this fresh concoction of green vegetables and mint. This makes a pretty starter and can be served in a small bowl or a large glass.

Heat a little oil in a large saucepan over a medium heat and fry the onion and garlic for a few minutes. Add the peas and stock, cover and cook for about 10 minutes, stirring frequently.

Remove the peas in stock from the heat and add the ice cubes – this helps to preserve the bright green colour. Transfer to a food processor and add the cucumbers. Season with salt, then blend until very smooth. If you are making this in advance, store it in the refrigerator until needed.

Serve in individual soup bowls or glasses and season each with a little salt and pepper, then add a nice dollop of crème fraîche and sprinkle with chopped mint.

ROASTED PEACH, HEIRLOOM TOMATO AND JAMBON DE BAYONNE SALAD

SERVES 4

3 red heritage beef (beefsteak)
  tomatoes (you can use 'Black
  Krim' or yellow as well)
olive oil, for cooking and drizzling
sunflower oil, for cooking
6 peaches, halved and de-stoned
150 g (3½ oz) air-dried Bayonne
  ham (or prosciutto)
juice of ½ lemon
fleur de sel and freshly ground
  black pepper
Greek basil leaves, to serve

Peach season is literally the dream in Provence. They come in white, yellow, flat or vineyard varieties and all of them are delicious. White peaches have a slightly more subtle, floral flavour, whereas yellow peaches are juicier and more full-on. The vineyard peach, which only appears here during high summer, has beautiful red flesh and tastes more akin to summer berries.

You can pretty much use any peach for this recipe, although I'd buy slightly firm ones, as otherwise they will quickly turn to mush on the griddle. I prefer to skin the tomatoes for this recipe, but you don't have to. You can add some burrata or buffalo mozzarella for an even more complete meal.

Prepare the tomatoes by plunging them into boiling water. Once the skins split, remove the tomatoes from the water and peel back the skins with a good paring knife. Cut them into even slices, then remove the seeds with the tip of a knife. Set aside on a platter.

Rub a griddle pan with a mixture of olive and sunflower oil, then put on the hob over a high heat. Lay the peaches on the hot griddle, cut-sides down, and let them caramelise for about 3 minutes, or until you can see the lines from the griddle in their flesh. Turn them over and grill the other sides – it will be less effective on the skin, but it adds to the flavour.

Slice the peach halves and arrange them randomly between the tomatoes on the platter. Tear up the ham and place it evenly over the peaches and tomatoes. Drizzle over some olive oil, squeeze over the lemon and sprinkle with some fleur de sel and a healthy grind of black pepper. Add plenty of the gorgeous small basil leaves (it's well worth adding a pot to your windowsill).

FENNEL AND PEAR SALAD WITH CRISPY SALMON SLICES

SERVES 4

2 fennel bulbs
oil (use half olive, half sunflower
    for cooking)
4 small salmon fillets
    (preferably skin-on)
3 pears (not too ripe), cored
    and thinly sliced lengthways
fleur de sel and freshly ground
    pink pepper

For the vinaigrette
3 tablespoons olive oil
juice of ½ lemon
1 teaspoon mayonnaise

One of my absolute favourite flavours is the combination of aromatic fennel and crunchy, sweet pear, and it pairs even more beautifully with a succulent slice of salmon. This is a light and aromatic summer recipe, perfect for an alfresco lunch. I like to quickly fry the fennel to bring out its flavour, but make sure it doesn't turn too soft.

Cut the fennel bulbs into thin slices and keep the fennel fronds growing out of the top. Chop the fronds finely and set them aside for the sauce.

Heat a little oil in a frying pan (skillet) over a medium heat and quickly fry off both sides of the fennel slices, then remove from the heat and season with some salt.

Make the vinaigrette by whisking together the olive oil, lemon juice, mayonnaise, a pinch of salt and the chopped fennel greens.

Wash and pat dry the salmon fillets and make sure any scales are removed from the skin by scraping it with a sharp knife. Heat a little oil in a frying pan over a high heat. Fry the salmon, skin-side down, for about 5–7 minutes to get it nice and crispy, then quickly finish off with a couple of minutes on the other side (if your salmon fillet is very thick, you may need to adapt your cooking time a little). Remove from the heat and leave the fillets in the warm pan, ideally covered.

Assemble the fennel and sliced pears on individual plates or a sharing platter, then add the salmon fillets on top. Spoon over the vinaigrette, season with some fleur de sel and pink pepper, and serve.

CHEAT'S DUCK CONFIT WITH PICKLED AND HONEY-GLAZED QUINCE

SERVES 4

4 heaped tablespoons caster (superfine) sugar

250 ml (8 fl oz/1 cup) water

250 ml (8 fl oz/1 cup) white wine vinegar

4 cloves

3 star anise

4 quinces (or very firm pears if not available)

½ lemon

4 tablespoons of clear honey

4 duck legs

frisée (curly endive) or red chicory (endive) salad, to serve

Quince – or *coing* – is the emblematic fruit of Cotignac, from which the village is said to derive its name. Each year towards the end of October, the 'Association of the Quince' comes together to celebrate the fruit in the traditional way, with a big village party of food stands, market stalls and a bouncy castle for the kids.

Quince requires a little prep – in the form of poaching, pickling or roasting – to bring out its fragrant, honeyed scent, but the effort is well worth it. In early autumn (fall), they become an excellent choice for serving with roast meats, whether it's a seared pork chop or a meltingly tender duck leg with crispy skin.

Put the sugar, water and vinegar into a saucepan and bring to the boil. Add the cloves and star anise. Peel and halve the quinces and rub them with the lemon to stop them browning. Lower the quinces into the sugar syrup and simmer for 25–45 minutes until tender.

Preheat the oven to 180°C fan (400°F).

When the quinces are tender, transfer them from the syrup to a baking dish or roasting tin. Measure out 150 ml (5 fl oz/scant ⅔ cup) of the cooking liquid, add the honey and pour over the quinces. Bake for 30 minutes, or until they are very soft, basting frequently.

In the meantime, place the duck legs, skin-side down, in a heavy-based frying pan (skillet) over a medium heat and cook for 10 minutes, or until the skin is browned all over. You may need to do this in batches.

Arrange the duck legs, skin-side up, in a large roasting tin, cover with foil and cook in the oven for 40 minutes, or until the flesh is tender and starting to come away from the bone. Increase the temperature to 200°C fan (425°F), remove the foil and cook for a further 20 minutes, or until the legs are cooked through and the skin is crisp.

Serve the duck legs with the quince and a dressed frisée or red chicory salad.

SAFFRON RISOTTO WITH CONFIT TOMATOES

SERVES 4

1–1.3 litres (34–44 fl oz/4–5 cups) good-quality chicken or vegetable stock
olive oil, for cooking
1 white onion, diced
240 g (8½ oz/generous 1 cup) arborio or carnaroli rice
100 ml (3½ fl oz/scant ½ cup) white or rosé wine
1 very generous pinch of saffron threads
50 g (1¾ oz) salted butter
100 g (3½oz) Parmesan, finely grated

FOR THE CONFIT TOMATOES

400 g (14 oz) cherry tomatoes, halved
a few sprigs of thyme or sage
75 ml (2½ fl oz/5 tablespoons) extra virgin olive oil

One of the most prized products of the upper Var is the elusive saffron – or, as it's locally known, *l'or rouge*. Harvested in the autumn (fall) months from the flowering crocus plant, the stems are handpicked and then dried. I love to flaunt the local delicacy in this vibrant risotto punctuated with sweet, slow-cooked cherry tomatoes.

Preheat the oven to 150°C fan (350°F).

First, make the confit tomatoes. Place them snugly in a high-sided baking tray (pan) with the thyme or sage and extra virgin olive oil. Bake for 30 minutes while the risotto is cooking.

Next, move on to the risotto. Heat the stock in a large saucepan over a medium heat and maintain it on a low simmer.

Heat a generous drizzle of olive oil in a deep frying pan (skillet) over a medium heat and fry the onion for 4–5 minutes until starting to soften, then add the rice. Toast the rice for 2 minutes, stirring regularly. When it looks translucent, add the wine. Cook the wine off for a minute or so, then add the saffron.

Next, start adding the stock, one ladleful at a time, stirring very regularly. Cook over a low heat for 20 minutes until the rice is still firm but cooked. Remove from the heat, then add the butter, cover and allow to rest for 2 minutes. Finally, stir in a generous handful of the Parmesan.

Remove the tomatoes from the oven. Divide the risotto between bowls, then top with the tomatoes and plenty of extra Parmesan.

LEMON MADELEINES WITH WHITE CHOCOLATE DIP

MAKES ABOUT 20

100 g (3½ oz/scant ½ cup)
  caster (superfine) sugar
zest of 1 unwaxed lemon
3 large eggs
20 g (¾ oz/1 tablespoon)
  clear honey
pinch of salt
150 g (5½ oz/scant 1¼ cups)
  T55 flour, plus extra for dusting
5 g (¼ oz/1 teaspoon)
  baking powder
125 g (4½ oz) unsalted butter,
  melted and cooled, plus
  extra for greasing

FOR THE DIP
150 g (5½ oz) good-quality white
  cooking chocolate, chopped
150 ml (5 fl oz/scant ⅔ cup)
  double (heavy) cream
50 ml (1¾ fl oz/3½ tablespoons)
  whole milk

Madeleines feel a little scary to make and you need to build in the time for the batter to chill if you want a great result, but once you have got the hang of it, they work a treat. You will need to invest in a good madeleine baking tin (pan) or silicone mould. This is a wonderful dessert for when you have kids over at a family lunch.

In a bowl, stir together the sugar and lemon zest. Add the eggs, honey and salt, and whisk until light and fluffy. Sift in the flour and baking powder, then mix gently until homogeneous. Add the cooled melted butter and mix gently. Cover and place in the refrigerator to rest overnight, or for at least 6 hours. Don't skip this part, as chilling the batter helps create the 'belly' on top of the madeleines.

When you're ready to bake, preheat the oven to 220°C fan (475°F).

Using a brush, grease a madeleine tray (pan) with butter, then dust with flour. Scoop tablespoons of the chilled batter into each mould.

Reduce the temperature of the oven to 200°C fan (425°F) and add the madeleines. After about 4 minutes, the belly of the madeleines will collapse (but it will come back). At this point, reduce the temperature again to 180°C fan (400°F) and bake for a further 5 minutes until golden.

Remove the madeleines from the oven and wait a few minutes for them to cool down before removing them from the tin safely and placing on a wire rack.

Put the chocolate into a heatproof bowl. In a small saucepan, heat the cream and milk over a medium heat until simmering – do not let it boil. Pour the cream mixture over the chocolate and stir gently until melted.

Enjoy the madeleines cold or warm, dipping them in the sauce.

THE VERY LONG APERITIF

When entertaining in the early evening, we'll often just serve drinks and a bevvy of finger foods in a relaxed setting, replacing a more formal dinner. It's a great way to be together without the inevitable running back and forth from the kitchen, and it feels more sociable and comfortable. Perfect for families, too, it means kids come and go and there is no huge stress about sitting down to eat.

The concept of this aperitif-dinner hybrid (*l'apéro dinatoire*) relies on making nibbles plentiful and pretty, with some healthy bits thrown in – a platter of crudités (sliced, raw vegetables) with dips always works well. Serve your more substantial nibbles, such as stuffed courgette (zucchini) flowers or mimosa eggs, on decorative platters with a little visual wow factor. Put out small plates so that everyone can take a few bits at a time. The addition of cheese and charcuterie, a spread of crostini, seeded crackers, nuts and olives means everyone will be happy mopping up the dips and tucking in.

Another nice touch is to start with a light cocktail, using fruit and herbaceous aromas to give it lots of flavour. One of my favourites is a strawberry and basil smash – make it with the spirit of your choice, plenty of ice and enjoy!

A refreshing granita, served in its own fruit shell, is a great way to finish on a light note – we love our melon one featured on page 63, it's so tasty and typical of the sweet flavours of summer.

STRAWBERRY, BASIL AND PINK PEPPER GIN SMASH

SERVES 4

120 ml (4 fl oz/½ cup) water
120 g (4½ oz) white caster
  (superfine) sugar
1 small bunch of basil leaves
125 g (4½ oz) strawberries,
  cleaned and halved
150 ml (5 fl oz/scant ⅔ cup)
  dry gin
ice cubes
sparkling water, to top

Strawberry and basil is such a brilliant combination and this is a really gorgeous light drink, perfect to start a summer evening in style.

First, make the basil syrup. Put the water and sugar into a saucepan and bring to the boil. Once the sugar has dissolved, remove the pan from the heat and allow to cool a little. Add about ten of the basil leaves and let them infuse for a few minutes, then remove the leaves. Let it cool completely.

Set aside eight strawberry halves, then put the rest into a cocktail shaker (or a jug/pitcher if you don't have one). Use a muddler to crush the strawberries.

Add the gin and crush the strawberries again to mix thoroughly and infuse. Next, add the basil syrup and top up with some ice cubes. Put the lid on the shaker and shake the mixture thoroughly (or stir it well if you're making it in a jug).

Put some ice into four wine glasses or tumblers and pour the gin smash through a cocktail strainer (or pour through a sieve/fine mesh strainer). Top up with sparkling water and very gently stir with a spoon to mix the ingredients without losing the bubbles. Decorate with a couple of strawberry halves and a leaf of basil to serve.

Note
For a naughtier version, top up with sparkling wine and just a splash of soda water.

CRISPY FENNEL SEED SOCCA WITH CARAMELISED ONIONS

SERVES 2–4 AS A SNACK

130 g (4½ oz/scant 1¼ cups) chickpea (gram) flour

240 ml (8¼ oz/1 cup) water

2 tablespoons extra virgin olive oil

olive oil, for cooking

2 red or white onions, thinly sliced

1 teaspoon fennel seeds

4 bushy sprigs of rosemary, leaves picked

flaky sea salt

In truly traditional style, socca, the gram flour-based Niçois flatbread, is best made in a wood-fired oven. The hot temperature allows it to cook in seconds and achieve crispy edges and a soft, custardy centre, but a hot pan and grill (broiler) does a good job, too. This salty snack is the perfect aperitif – quick to make and excellent with a glass of rosé. A little pecorino grated over the top is also worth a try! You can make the mixture 24 hours ahead and keep it in the refrigerator until needed.

Combine the chickpea flour, water, extra virgin olive oil and a pinch of salt in a bowl and whisk to combine, making sure there are no lumps.

Heat a glug of olive oil in a well-cured cast-iron frying pan (skillet) over a medium heat (or use an ovenproof non-stick pan). Add the onions and a pinch of salt and fry for 7–8 minutes until they colour but aren't too soft (a little bite is good). Add the fennel seeds and toast for 1 minute until fragrant. Remove the onions and fennel seeds from the pan and set aside.

Preheat your grill (broiler) to high.

Heat the pan once more over a high heat (or at this point you'd be adding it to your hot wood-fired oven) and cover the base of the pan with a thick layer of oil. When it's red hot, add half the batter and swirl to cover the base – the edges and base should sizzle and get really crispy. Scatter with plenty of salt and the rosemary. Once the base is set, after 1–2 minutes, add half the onions and fennel seeds. Slide the pan under the grill to finish cooking on top. Serve immediately, cut into triangles, then repeat with the remaining batter and onion topping.

STUFFED COURGETTE FLOWERS WITH FRESH GOAT'S CHEESE, LEMON, HONEY AND BASIL

SERVES 4

8 courgette (zucchini) flowers
  (courgettes attached
  if available)
200 g (7 oz) soft fresh
  goat's cheese
zest of 1 unwaxed lemon
1 handful of basil, leaves
  chopped or torn, plus a few
  extra bushy sprigs
8 chives
salt and freshly ground
  black pepper

**FOR THE BATTER
AND FRYING**
1 litre (34 fl oz/4⅓ cups)
  neutral oil
1 large egg
150ml (5 fl oz/scant ⅔ cup)
  ice-cold sparkling water
120 g (4¼ oz/scant 1 cup) plain
  (all-purpose) flour, sifted

TO SERVE
clear honey
lemon juice

As early as April, the courgette (zucchini) flowers start to make their first appearances in the market stalls in town, around the same time as the fields and roadsides fill with wildflowers, poppies, lilacs and flowering rosemary and thyme, making it one of the prettiest times to be in Provence.

This recipe borrows a couple of other nation's techniques – a light tempura batter from Japan and the stuffing of courgette flowers from Italy – yet it couldn't be more fitting for the area, where the flowers grow like weeds. After the flowers are stuffed, crisped and fried, I like to drizzle them with a little of the local honey.

Remove the stigmas from inside the courgette flowers, trying as best you can to keep the flowers intact.

Combine the goat's cheese, lemon zest, chopped or torn basil and a generous amount of seasoning in a bowl and mix well. Use a teaspoon to spoon the goat's cheese mixture into the flowers, pressing it in firmly. Twist the end of the flower and tie a chive around the end to secure the stuffing. Set aside.

Pour the frying oil into a heavy-based saucepan and bring to a medium-high heat.

Beat the egg with the ice-cold water in a bowl until smooth, then add the flour and whisk until there are no lumps remaining. You want the mixture to be thick enough to coat the flowers. Drip a little of the batter into the oil. If it floats straight away and sizzles enthusiastically, you are ready to fry. Line a tray with paper towels.

Drag the courgette flowers through the batter and then drop them carefully into the oil. Depending on the size of the pan, you can fry three or four at a time, but don't overcrowd the pan or the temperature of the oil will drop too quickly. Cook for 2 minutes on each side, until the batter is crispy, then transfer to the lined tray and repeat with the remaining flowers. Drag the remaining bushy basil sprigs through the batter and fry until crisp.

Serve straight away with an extra sprinkle of salt, a drizzle of honey and a few squeezes of lemon juice.

SPICY MIMOSA EGGS WITH CRISPY SAGE

SERVES 4

4 eggs
1½ tablespoons mayonnaise
1 teaspoon Dijon mustard
a sprinkle of cayenne pepper
    (or more if you like
    them spicier)
3 tablespoons unsalted butter
8 small–medium sage leaves
salt and freshly ground
    black pepper
pinch of cayenne pepper

I have a huge nostalgic love for this French classic – it takes me right back to my mum making it for dinner parties in the 1970s. They are chic again, which is great news, and here is a version with a herbaceous sage twist.

Bring a saucepan of water to the boil and gently add the eggs. Cook for 10 minutes, then transfer the eggs to a bowl of ice-cold water and allow to cool completely. Once cool, peel them and halve them lengthways.

Remove the yolks with a teaspoon and place them in a bowl. Add the mayonnaise, mustard and cayenne pepper and season with salt and pepper. Mix until creamy, then adjust the seasoning, if needed.

Pipe or spoon the mixture back into the egg whites and keep in the refrigerator.

Melt the butter in a small frying pan (skillet) over a medium heat. Add the sage leaves and cook until the butter starts to foam and turn golden. Remove the pan from the heat and transfer the crispy sage to a plate lined with paper towels.

Arrange the eggs on a serving platter and garnish them with the crispy sage leaves, a pinch of cayenne pepper, then drizzle them with some sage-infused brown butter, if you like.

CANTALOUPE MELON AND LIME GRANITA

SERVES 4

100 g (3½ oz/scant ½ cup)
  caster (superfine) sugar
100 ml (3½ fl oz/scant ½ cup)
  water
2 cantaloupe melons
juice of 2 limes plus zest of 1

Simple and refreshing, this cantaloupe granita is summer in a melon bowl. The perfect end to a relaxed lunch together or to be served in the afternoon by the pool.

Place the sugar and water in a saucepan and bring to a simmer to dissolve the sugar. Once the sugar has dissolved, remove from the heat and set aside to cool.

Cut the melons in half through the 'waist' and scoop out the seeds and discard them, then scoop out most of the flesh into the bowl of a food processor. Leave a wall of flesh inside the melon, about 1 cm (½ in) thick (so not scooping out right to the skin). Blend the flesh, adding the cool sugar syrup and the lime juice and zest. Reserve the hollowed-out melons, because these will be used as bowls for the granita.

Pour the blended melon into a container or baking dish that will fit in the freezer. Place the four cantaloupe shells in the freezer too. Freeze for 1 hour, then use a fork to scrape the granita mixture. Freeze again and then scrape again. Repeat this two or three times until you have a granita texture.

Transfer the granita to the cantaloupe halves to serve.

LIVING THE VILLAGE LIFE

To our surprise, life in our little village turned out to be anything but boring. We soon realised that you cannot get across the main square without spending at least 15 minutes saying hello to everyone, planting a lot of kisses (*bises*) on cheeks along the way and catching up with bits of gossip and news. The clocks here really tick more slowly, and people take time to talk to each other. Everyone knows you and everyone knows your children. I would get told what mine were up to as soon as my back was turned. But we could also be certain that if one of them was in trouble, someone would be there to help. I loved that my kids were free to walk around the village, go to the playground or to their friends' houses on foot.

As soon as the evenings get warmer in spring, the village comes to life and people meet outdoors for an aperitif (*l'apéro*) and some food. Weekends are dominated by themed events, specialist markets and musical entertainment. There is also a lively art scene in Cotignac (like in many other villages in Provence) that has drawn artists from all over the world to settle. One of the reasons is the beautiful landscape, but also the light that is well known to feel so special around here.

Music is another great pillar of French village life, and there will be frequent concerts in the street, especially so on Midsummer's Eve, which is 'La Fête de la Musique', where the whole village erupts into spontaneous song. Sitting in one of the restaurants on the square and eating a nice platter of cheese and charcuterie while listening to someone making music is still one of my favourite moments.

Another pleasure of living here is that antique fairs (*brocantes*) and flea markets frequently pop up on our squares and by the roadside. You can get out to hunt for original and fun pieces, especially if you go early in the day. Our friends Cathy and Peter Bullen, who have lived on and off in Cotignac for more than 30 years, are another couple who turned their passion into their livelihood. They now run a series of lively village fetes back in their native Suffolk and bring their treasures from Provence over to the UK. It's a lovely feeling to find a bargain that will fill a special spot in your house and that is often unique and pre-loved.

BROCANTING IN PROVENCE

~

BY CATHY BULLEN

Seeking out decorative treasures is a joy, but be warned – brocanting in Provence can quickly become an addiction! Follow the plane tree avenues that line so many Provençal routes and you'll spot homemade and battered signs nailed to a post, or else garish out-of-place neon posters, all announcing a local brocante (antique market) or vide-grenier (flea market). Follow these and you'll be led into the real Provence: however, don't be dreaming of French pastel perfection, these markets are flooded with colour, grime, life, laughter and, most importantly, a wealth of discarded decorative treasures!

In an age when upcycling pre-loved pieces is very much aligned with us living a more environmentally conscious life, there's nowhere better to seek out on-trend vintage and antique pieces than France. Why, you ask? Simply because the French have a culture steeped in the appreciation and creation of innovative style and design, so the brocante is the perfect destination for seeking out fabulous decorative pieces from every style and époque.

Before you begin your adventure, you have several decisions to make, largely dependent on your time, your purse and the type of experience you enjoy. Firstly, do you want to potter, basket in hand, searching for that something special, or is this a targeted endeavour to fill up your van with treasures? This may determine whether you want to visit a large, established city brocante, brimming with a big choice of stalls (most large towns have weekly or monthly events that are published on regional websites). Or, are you happy to take your luck with what a small local event may offer?

Undoubtedly, both large and small brocantes offer their own charm – a large event will sing with the sound of haggling, where dealers know the value of their stock and want to get the best price for their pieces. There'll be an array of choice, prices and styles, with fakes and fortune to be found: this is the choice for you

'We love to gather pieces and link their decorative narrative through an identified colour scheme.'

if you want to be sure of a good selection and definitely want to buy.

For us, however, the small *brocante* has long ago stolen our hearts – once flowing with original antiques brought down from an attic clearance (hence the name *vide-grenier*, which means 'empty attic'), a small local market unearths a very mixed bunch of pre-loved pieces. However, it's still the place to spot a true treasure, a discarded piece, the value of which is yet undetected, no longer loved by its owner, but something to make your own heart sing.

Wherever you decide to venture, the key rule of brocanting remains much the same: arrive early! If you're keen to spot a unique piece, you'll need to rub shoulders with the professional dealers who will be waiting with torches for dawn to break and for the stallholders to bring out their stock. Always ensure you bring along a purse bursting with cash – you'll spot something you just can't leave without, and card readers are not always an option. Etiquette is equally important, and any interaction needs to open with a smile and '*bonjour*' if you hope to haggle.

Haggling is a slightly intuitive pursuit. No one wants to pay over the odds for anything, and where and what hour you're antique hunting can affect the initial price suggested. So, step carefully into the world of haggling. A dealer will

feel insulted if you immediately slash the price in half, however there's usually a little haggling expected as it's all part of the game – a bit of banter can bring fun and laughter into the sale and make your purchase even more memorable when you get it home.

The joy of finding that special piece is euphoric, especially if you've been trawling through a dusty box of unloved treasures when it catches your eye. Our most exciting buys are not always the most valuable, but they've been things in which we've been able to spot original style, truly authentic pieces that we've been able to upcycle, adding unique flair to our home. The beauty of decorating is that 'mix and match' is so on trend and almost anything goes, as long as it's loved by its owner, ensuring every style and era work together. We love to gather pieces and link their decorative narrative through an identified colour scheme. Remember, colour glows in Provence: it is the gift of blue skies and golden sunlight and is embraced in almost all the artisanal treasures you'll find on your brocanting adventures – so be brave and enjoy the moment.

THE SPORT OF PROVENCE: PÉTANQUE

Playing boules, called *pétanque* here in the South, is a favourite pastime that is undertaken with a lot of competitive spirit. It's great fun to watch the various generations of the village meet on the boules court with deadly seriousness. Your fellow boule-ist is called your 'adversary' for good reason, and there are no less than 12 pages of official rules that you must supposedly follow. After a while watching the locals battle on the boules court, you know better than to be perturbed by the loud shouting and obsessive measuring of distances, followed by the hugs and celebrations of the winning team. Playing *pétanque* also inevitably involves sliced sausage, olives, a glass of pastis and some chilled rosé being poured, occasionally culminating in a full on-court meal after play.

Here are a few tips so you can pass for someone who vaguely knows what they are doing! Firstly, hold the ball correctly with the hand covering the ball, take a slow swing back with your arm, accelerating forwards and releasing the ball at the right moment, trying to get it close to the *cochonnet*, which is the name for the small, coloured ball that's the jack. I am sure that throwing it with your hand placed below the ball gives you away as an amateur – even if it is 'legal' – and I did this for years. No real shame I figured, though – it's the result that counts.

The beauty of a game of *pétanque* is that it can be played by all ages and abilities. Done best with a drink in hand, which also helps overcome any worry about the level of your game, or the need to speak French to the locals. It's a naturally social occasion, where we chat when it's not our turn to play, and it's the perfect pre-dinner activity in Provence.

If you're in France, you may be lucky enough to have a court by your holiday home or B&B, so go and make the most of it with family and friends! We always play when we have visitors, even if they are here for business – it relaxes everyone and there are always many laughs. Here you can see us playing a few games at the historic Hôtel Lou Calen in Cotignac and indulging in some rosé and easy snacks. Over the next few pages, I will show you some fun foods to share courtside.

FAMILY-STYLE RULES OF PÉTANQUE:

~

1. The game is played between two teams with one, two or three players. In singles or doubles each player uses three boules, in triples reduce the number of boules to two per competitor.

2. Make sure you have identified your boules balls and that their markings are identical.

3. Toss a coin to decide who starts and gets to throw the jack (*le cochonnet*).

4. Draw a circle of around 50cm in diameter, within which each player must remain when throwing the boule ball.

5. The winner of the coin toss throws the *cochonnet* between 4m and 8m (or 6 to 10 paces) from the circle in any direction – make sure to avoid the court boundary by less than 1m, otherwise throw again.

6. Any player from the coin-toss-winning team then throws the first boule. Your aim is to get as close as possible to the *cochonnet* without touching it.

7. A player from the opposing team(s) then steps into the circle. Their goal is to throw their boule closer to the *cochonnet* than their opponent. Or to knock the opponent's boule further away. '*Tu tires ou tu pointes*', the classic courtside question refers to whether you are trying to shoot at your opponent's boule, or aiming for the *cochonnet*.

8. Once all boules are thrown, identify whose ball is nearest to the *cochonnet*, you may find a tape measure handy if it's not glaringly obvious. One point is given for each boule ball that is closer than any of the opposing team's balls.

9. The winning team gets to start the next round.

10. The overall winner is whoever reaches 13 points first. Extensive celebrations are encouraged!

COURGETTE, TOMME AND COPPA MINI BROCHETTES

SERVES 4

olive oil, for cooking
2 small courgettes (zucchini),
    sliced into 1.5 cm (½ in)
    rounds
150 g (5½ oz) coppa, sliced
    in half
350 g (12 oz) tomme (or another
    hard cheese), cut into 2 cm
    (¾ in) cubes

A lovely snack or aperitif sharing dish. Tomme is a French semi-hard mountain cheese, but you can replace it with any nice cheese that you can cut into cubes. These brochettes should be small so that they can be eaten in one or two bites.

Heat a little oil in a saucepan over a high heat and brown the courgette slices on each side, then remove from the pan so they don't become soggy. Cut the rounds into quarters.

Thread a slice of folded coppa onto a wooden cocktail stick (toothpick), then add a cube of cheese, followed by a piece of courgette, then repeat. Lay the sticks on a wooden board or rustic plate, ready to chomp.

ROSÉ-SOAKED PICKLES

MAKES I X 800 ML
(27 FL OZ) JAR

200–250 ml (7–8½ fl oz/scant
   1–1 cup) rosé (or white) wine
120 ml (4 fl oz/½ cup) distilled
   white vinegar
50 g (1¾ oz/scant ¼ cup)
   caster (superfine) sugar
3 garlic cloves, peeled but
   left whole
5 pink peppercorns
1 tablespoon salt
herbs of your choice, such as
   rosemary, thyme and/or
   bay leaves
vegetables of your choice, such
   as radishes, red onions, French
   beans and/or cucumber, sliced.
   Use approximately 450 g
   (1 lb) of vegetables.

A fun way to use up any leftover rosé (or white wine), these super delicious crunchy pickled vegetables are perfect as part of an aperitif or snack. For the best visual effect, leave them in the pickling jar for your guests to help themselves.

Preheat the oven to 140°C fan (325°F) and place an 800 ml (27 fl oz) jar inside for 10 minutes to sterilise it.

In a saucepan, combine the rosé, vinegar, sugar, garlic, peppercorns, salt and herbs. Bring to the boil and stir until the sugar dissolves. Adjust the flavours, if needed.

Put the sliced vegetables into the jar and pour over the pickling liquid to the top, ensuring the vegetables are fully submerged. Make sure you add the garlic, peppercorns and herbs. Leave to cool, then cover with the lid and keep in the refrigerator.

Refrigerate for at least 24 hours before eating (they will keep for up to 2 months).

STEAMED ARTICHOKES WITH WHIPPED ANCHOÏADE

SERVES 4

4 globe or large artichokes
juice of 1 lemon

FOR THE WHIPPED ANCHOÏADE

1 small garlic clove,
   roughly chopped
1 teaspoon Dijon mustard
1 large egg yolk
15 anchovy fillets
50 ml (1¾ fl oz/3½ tablespoons)
   extra virgin olive oil
50 ml (1¾ fl oz/3½ tablespoons)
   vegetable oil
2 tablespoons lemon juice,
   or more to taste

While you shouldn't really mess with a recipe that is steeped in Provençal culture and cuisine, there is something to be said for whipping up anchoïade into a velvety textured dip. The traditional recipe is a coarse paste, bashed in a pestle and mortar, perhaps with the addition of a sprinkling of capers. But the silkiness of this version, for me, makes it extra appealing, and an excellent counterpart to the metallic sweetness of a steamed artichoke.

These make the perfect snack to bring down to the *pétanque* court.

Start by preparing each artichoke. Trim the stem so that it sits flat, then remove any smaller leaves towards the base and trim about 1–2 cm (½–¾ in) off the top to get rid of the prickly tips, or if there aren't any, leave it as it is. Next, use a paring knife to peel away the tougher outer leaves, then peel away the rougher green skin around the stalk. Rub the white flesh with lemon juice to stop it discolouring.

Place the artichokes in a steamer basket over a pan of boiling water and steam for about 15–30 minutes, depending on their size, until you can easily pull away a leaf.

For the whipped anchoïade, put the garlic, mustard, egg yolk and anchovy fillets into a food processor and blend together. Add 1 tablespoon of the oils at a time, blending between additions, until you have a thick paste. Keep going until it's all incorporated and perfectly smooth, then add the lemon juice and blend again.

Serve the steamed artichokes with the anchoïade for dipping the leaves into. Once all the leaves are gone, scoop out the inner hairy chokes and discard them (this can't be done until the leaves are soft from the steaming) and slice the hearts to serve with the remaining dip.

NINA'S LEMON AND ALMOND TART

SERVES 8

Makes one 25 cm (10 in) cake

FOR THE PASTRY

200 g (7 oz/1²/₃ cups) cake
   and pastry flour, plus extra
   for dusting
50 g (1¾ oz/scant ¼ cup)
   caster (superfine) sugar
pinch of salt
100 g (3½ oz) cold unsalted
   butter, cubed, plus extra
   for greasing

FOR THE FILLING

75 g (23/4 oz) unsalted butter
120 g (4¼ oz/scant 1¼ cups)
   ground almonds (almond meal)
200 g (7 oz/scant 1 cup) caster
   (superfine) sugar
zest and juice of 2 unwaxed
   lemons
4 large eggs
icing (powdered) sugar,
   for dusting

Isabelle, also known as Nina, is a personality in our village. She runs a small restaurant, serving mainly Italian-inspired food. Everything is homemade and the menu is small and well-curated. She and her husband also run an antiques business, so she has a huge stash of decorative items in her restaurant. You will eat off lovely mismatched vintage plates, old monogrammed linen tablecloths and water will be served in eye-catching decanters. No one has ever left her restaurant hungry; there is a real sense of generosity and of making the most of the pleasurable moment.

First, make the pastry. You can make this in a stand mixer or by hand. Place the flour in a mound on a cool work surface and add the sugar and salt. Then, gradually add the butter, working it in with your fingertips. Add just enough water to bring it together into a dough, then form it into a ball and put it into a lidded container. If using a stand mixer, use your dough hook and proceed in the same order of the recipe, adding the butter cubes in a few steps. Knead the dough for a couple of minutes, then follow the last step by hand. Cover and leave to rest in the refrigerator for at least 1 hour.

Preheat the oven to 175°C fan (385°F) and grease a 25 cm (10 in) non-stick tart tin (pan).

Once rested, roll out the pastry on a floured work surface, then press it into the prepared tin. Prick the pastry with a fork, line it with baking parchment and fill with baking beans (or small, clean pebbles). Blind bake in the oven for 15 minutes.

While the pastry base is in the oven, prepare the filling. Soften the butter in an ovenproof bowl set over a saucepan of simmering water, or in the microwave on low, then place in a bowl or stand mixer. Add the ground almonds, sugar, lemon zest and juice and eggs, and whisk well.

Remove the pastry from the oven and take out the baking parchment and weights. Pour the filling into the pastry case and return to the oven for 15–20 minutes until it's set. Remove from the oven and allow to cool, then carefully remove from the tin and dust with icing sugar.

THE VINES

LES VIGNES

LOST AND FOUND

You could say we were sometimes a little lost in Provence. But we also found some rather special things, often when we weren't really looking. While we were busy searching for a family house, we also hunted for a vineyard to grow our own vines. We had already spent some years working with a small selection of local farmers to make wine, but of course the desire to have our feet in our own soil never quite left us. Yet, as we had already been taught on several occasions, good things take time in Provence.

We looked at nearly 40 vineyards of all shapes and sizes, and had a very lengthy, but ultimately unsuccessful, attempt to purchase an estate very near our house in Cotignac. As hope for this project came to an end, Stephen said there was one more place for us to see. I eventually relented to drive downhill to the nature reserve at the foothills of the Maures mountain range, to view the curiously named 'Domaine de L'Amour'. Unexpectedly, as we drove off the main road, down a rickety path and through a simple iron gate, an ochre bastide with blue shutters appeared in the distance. We locked eyes and knew this one had to be ours. The Domaine de L'Amour was really love at first sight. After some negotiations with the owner, he decided we were to be his buyers, and following a firm handshake and many formalities later, this bijou place became ours. We both felt like this little gem had been quietly lying in wait for us to turn it into the haven of biodiversity and beautiful wilderness that it is today.

BACK TO NATURE

Initially, I had to keep my instinct to get busy in the houses on the estate in check, as investment in the vineyard had to come first. Meanwhile, Stephen threw himself into intense research on various farming methods. We knew we wanted to farm organically, but we were looking for an even more considered way of working the land. A Cotignac neighbour told us about a podcast by Mimi Casteel, a biologist turned wine farmer from Oregon, who talked about the concept of regenerative viticulture. It didn't take long for us to be convinced enough to try our hand. The idea that you can heal the soil — and ours needed healing — and put back more than you take out was just so appealing. But we also knew there were risks. We're located in a very dry area, and a full harvest is far from guaranteed most years. Introducing competition in the form of other plants that take up precious water was the opposite of what is practiced here in many vineyards, where bare earth is the norm. But we were determined to have a go and challenge ourselves to see what was possible and to potentially provide a place to learn for other farmers, too. The great news was that, if it worked, there were so many upsides. From a lower carbon footprint and higher levels of biodiversity to better grape quality, which of course equals better wine, this way of working promised to be a big improvement to what was done here before.

KEEP KISSING THE GROUND

The central tenet of regenerative agriculture is that the soil is the holy grail of your farming journey. Beautifully told by Woody Harrelson in the documentary, *Kiss the Ground*, it's also a perfectly logical idea, but it has been forgotten in the days of easy fertilisers and huge tractors. Plants need living soils to get the nutrients they require to produce tasty, nutritious fruit and vegetables. Once you understand what happens below ground, with bugs, worms and fungi all working together to give each other what they need, it's clear that, as farmers, we must work to get this system back into balance.

A year after our purchase, we energetically set off on our journey to bring life back into our vineyard. We did this by adding beneficial plants and compost, planting trees and creating havens for wildlife. The difference after nearly four years of farming in this way is there for all to see and hear. The birdsong is almost deafening and bees busily feast on the many pollinator plants we've added. The soil is darker and denser; where before there was only compacted dirt, there is now life. It's been the most gratifying part of our Provençal journey, to have revitalised this beautiful paradise, and yet knowing we'll be making some great bottles of wine from it, too.

OUR LITTLE FARM

Animals are an important part of regenerative agriculture, and we loved the idea of having some at the farm. For an easy start, we bought some chickens and a couple of runner ducks. Then, a friend gave us some pigs and I fulfilled my secret wish to own a couple of alpacas. I found a pair of boys, one with striking blue eyes whom we named Vince, and his friend, Pablo. They are naturally funny, but you are well advised to make a wide berth around their hind legs! They happily roam the vineyard, grazing on what they find for most of the year. After a few weeks, someone brought us an orphaned dwarf goat called Zoë, who moved in with the alpacas. She's the undisputed farmyard boss and can often be found looking down at you from a tree. Between them, they eat all our food waste, provide some valuable compost for the vegetable garden and graze on our cover crop. The flock of chickens and ducks are busy turning over our compost heap and provide us with fresh eggs, perfect for our Domaine kitchen.

We've also started to experiment with a special row of vines that are trained over a pergola and in their semi-shade we grow other vegetables, like tomatoes, beans, courgettes (zucchini) and delicious melons. We call this our 'edible vineyard', and it's amazing how we can plant and harvest at several levels, making use of the most heat-resistant plants to help us grow more sensitive ones below. There is nothing more satisfying than picking our own sweet-tasting tomatoes and just eating them there and then, with a glug of good oil, salt and some freshly toasted bread. We're delighted when we can serve our visitors some homegrown produce, and the smile on their faces proves how delicious these sun-drenched fruit and vegetables are.

ROASTED CHARENTAIS MELON AND BURRATA WITH ESPELETTE PEPPER VINAIGRETTE

SERVES 4 AS A STARTER/SHARING PLATE

4 tablespoons olive oil, plus extra
   for roasting the melon
1 medium–large Charentais
   melon, sliced and rind removed
juice of ½ Lemon
pinch of Espelette pepper
   (or cayenne or Aleppo pepper),
   plus extra to taste
splash of red wine vinegar
pinch of light brown sugar
pinch of fleur de sel, plus extra
   to taste
1 ball of burrata

A delicious recipe that infuses sweet melon with a caramelised aroma, working brilliantly with the creaminess of the burrata and offset by the gentle spice of a piment d'Espelette vinaigrette. This French chilli spice is grown in the Basque country and is widely used in Provençal cuisine. If you don't have any, you can replace it with cayenne or Aleppo pepper.

Heat some oil in a frying pan (skillet) or griddle over a medium heat. Roast the melon slices for a couple of minutes on each side until slightly browned, being careful not to burn them (it happens quickly as they contain natural sugar). Remove from the pan and set aside to cool.

Make a vinaigrette by stirring together the 4 tablespoons of olive oil, lemon juice, Espelette pepper, vinegar, sugar and salt in a bowl.

Lay out the melon slices on their side on a serving dish, then tear up the burrata and scatter among the melon slices. Stir the vinaigrette again, then spoon it over the melon, making sure all the slices are nicely covered. Add some extra flakes of salt and Espelette pepper, depending on how much spice you enjoy.

TOMATES PROVENÇALE REVISITED, WITH GARLICKY PANGRATTATO AND CRISPY CAPERS

SERVES 4

4 large, best-quality beef
(beefsteak) tomatoes
extra virgin olive oil, for drizzling
4 tablespoons fresh breadcrumbs
2 garlic cloves, grated
1 tablespoon capers
a few sprigs of basil (purple
works well)
salt

Tomatoes are up there as one of the most widely used ingredients in the Provençal culinary repertoire, and that's completely fine by me. A simple, but aromatic dish, *tomates Provençale* comes baked until squishy in garlicky breadcrumbs and parsley. It's a simpler vegetarian variation on the ever-popular *tomates farcies*, which are hollowed out and stuffed with minced meat and also breadcrumbs. This vegetarian version is perfect for when tomatoes are at their peak and best eaten as they come.

Start by slicing the tomatoes. I like to do them almost Hasselback-style, leaving the base intact but opening up the tomato like a book. Using a very sharp knife or a tomato knife, slice the tomato thinly right down to about 1 cm (½ in) from the bottom so that the tomato opens out. Repeat with the other tomatoes. Place in a wide, shallow dish and scatter with salt and drizzle with plenty of olive oil. Leave for about 15 minutes.

Heat a layer of olive oil in a frying pan (skillet) over a medium heat. Add the breadcrumbs and cook for 2 minutes, then add the grated garlic and cook for a further 2 minutes until golden. Remove from the pan, then add another layer of olive oil. Drain the capers on paper towels, pat dry and add to the hot oil. Cook for 2 minutes, or until very crispy. Drain on paper towels and assemble the dish.

Place the tomatoes on a serving plate along with all their juices and scatter with the breadcrumbs and the crispy capers. Lay a few sprigs of basil over the top and serve.

PROVENÇAL PANZANELLA

SERVES 4–6

2 courgettes (zucchini),
  cut into strips
olive oil, for drizzling
1 tablespoon maple syrup
  (or agave nectar)
handful of pine nuts
½ leftover baguette or 1 large
  slice of sourdough
2–3 heirloom tomatoes
1 small head of Castelfranco
  (or other crunchy) lettuce,
  leaves torn
1 bunch of radishes, halved
10 anchovy fillets
bunch of basil leaves, torn
fleur de sel

FOR THE DRESSING
3 tablespoons olive oil
2 tablespoons maple syrup
juice of ½ lemon

A great, easy-to-assemble summer dish that makes good use of leftover bread and is full of colourful vegetables. This is lovely as part of a big lunch table or for a family barbecue to accompany grilled meats.

Preheat the oven to 180°C fan (400°F).

Place the courgette strips on a baking tray (pan) lined with parchment paper, then drizzle with olive oil and maple syrup. Sprinkle with salt and the pine nuts, then cook in the oven for 20 minutes, remove and set aside.

Put the leftover bread onto a separate tray and toast in the oven for a few minutes until crunchy all over (if it's quite hard to begin with, dampen it a little with water on the outside before putting it in the oven). Remove from the oven and cut into chunks, then leave to cool.

Slice the tomatoes, remove the stem scar and drain off the juice and seeds.

In a large bowl, mix all the dressing ingredients, then add the bread pieces and toss so that they are evenly coated (add more olive oil if necessary).

Place the courgettes and pine nuts, tomatoes, lettuce and radishes in the salad bowl and very gently turn to coat everything with the dressing.

Place anchovies over the top, tear up the basil, add a pinch of salt, and finally drizzle with a little bit more olive oil.

MAKING A FARMHOUSE A HOME

After we'd taken care of the most urgent projects in the vines, I was hugely excited to renovate and restore the houses on the estate. The main house, La Bastide, was in need of a big refresh and I was already renovating one of the outbuildings to turn it into a professional kitchen with a big wood-fired oven – perfect for roasting meats at high temperatures and for making *fougasse*, a traditional savoury snack with various fillings.

The main house is a rustic and spacious country mansion, originally dating from 1819. It had lots of potential to be brought back from the practical but uninspiring interiors that had been put in over the years. I was delighted that the floors were decked out in a simple but nice terracotta tile, which we were able to keep – and that was a big win! I set about updating the whole house over the next two years, reworking certain rooms more extensively, as well as re-tiling and refurbishing all six bathrooms. My aim was to bring a more

modern feel, while keeping as many original materials as possible. So, naturally, I started by working out what I could reuse. A lot of items would need repainting and repairing, but luckily there were a few keepers. Among them was an original roll-top bath, a nod to former owners who were English and who had brought it over in the 1970s. True to the fashion of those days, it was avocado green, so I painted it a soft pink instead and it has become the centrepiece of the suite now called *La Baignoire Rose*.

On that note, it's always useful to find the centrepiece of any room and then work around it, be that a piece of furniture, an amazing painting or other art object. It can not only show you the colour scheme that you'll need to adopt to complement it, but also determines whether you need to add more visual details, or dial things back a bit. My local gallerists, Simon and John, helped me source original paintings, and each room has a distinct colour scheme that took inspiration from our surroundings and the local flora. We feature rich yellows, burnt umber, shades of blue as a nod to the sea and accents of joyful corals and pinks. The original art is accompanied by framed old posters, vintage black-and-white photography and *brocante* finds. I found vases and jugs at local ceramicists' studios and ordered a big set of crockery from my favourite French earthenware producer. It's rough enamelled stoneware, so while precious and decorative it's also helpfully resistant to

chips and heat. Natural fabrics, such as washed linen, flax and cottons work best in these spaces, with some silk and embroidery where we needed a special touch.

However, being a keen cook, the most important room for me is of course the kitchen. I threw caution to the wind and painted it in a coat of creamy pink. Offset with a white marble work surface and black wrought-iron handles, it has turned out surprisingly calming and modern. The handmade Moroccan zellige-tiled splashback, finished with an all-round shelf above, is set in a rickety herringbone pattern. I enjoy pairing pale pinks with terracotta tones, so there are plenty of local bowls, jugs and platters lining the open alcoves to bring back a rustic touch. It's become the warm communal space I dreamed of, where we cook together while discussing of all sorts of things, and someone's always pouring a glass of rosé or mixing a delicious cocktail on the counter.

VIGNERONS APÉRO BOARD

SERVES 6 FOR GENEROUS NIBBLES

1 bunch of red grapes

olive oil, for drizzling

crunchy radishes

comté (or another similar hard cheese)

ripe brie or sheep's cheese

roasted walnuts and/or almonds

green or black olives in oil

dried figs or dates

saucisson (or another air-dried salami)

Bayonne ham (or another lean, dried ham)

breadsticks and slices of toasted sourdough brad

salt

This is served to every person invited to our Domaine and it always has the desired effect. People love to see the intricately arranged patterns of snacks on a large wooden board, with the roasted grapes at the centre – it's a wine lover's dream.

What you put on it is up to you, but here are some suggestions from us. It's also a great way to neatly use up any vegetables if they are still crunchy, or cheese or charcuterie. You do not need all of the below and feel free to swap out ingredients.

Preheat the oven to 180°C fan (400°F).

Coat the grapes in some olive oil and sprinkle them with salt. Place in a baking dish and bake in the oven for about 20 minutes until they are caramelised, being careful not to let them burn.

Meanwhile, build the apéro board. Leave space on the board free for a dish to receive the grapes once they are baked, as they will still lose some juice. Arrange all the ingredients in segments, ensuring that you make nice, neat patterns. Remove the grapes from the oven and place on a dish or on parchment paper.

Give your guests a very small plate, a napkin and a reusable mini fork (or cocktail sticks/toothpicks) to serve and re-serve themselves easily. Sit in a nice spot and pour out a glass of wine – there isn't a much nicer slow moment than this.

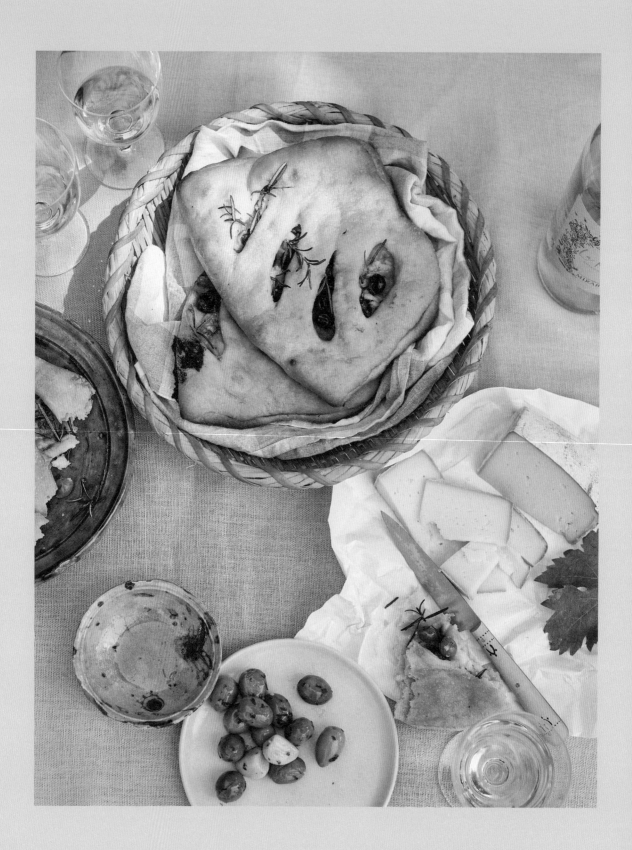

GOAT'S CHEESE, GRAPE AND ROSEMARY FOUGASSE

MAKES 4

500 g (1 lb 2 oz/4 cups) strong
    white bread flour
2 teaspoons fast-action yeast
1½ teaspoons fine salt
½ teaspoon caster (superfine)
    sugar
200–300 ml (7–10 fl oz/scant
    1–1¼ cups) warm water
olive oil, for brushing and greasing
8 sprigs of rosemary
150 g (5½ oz) firm, soft
    goat's cheese
200 g (7 oz) muscat grapes
    (or other small, sweet grapes)

A tear-and-share bread that's both savoury and sweet, this *fougasse* is the ideal harvest-table accompaniment. I prefer to use little muscat grapes, with thick skins but large pips, but any other small, sweet grape will work well.

Put the flour, yeast, salt and sugar into a stand mixer fitted with the dough hook attachment. Add 200 ml (7 fl oz/scant 1 cup) of the water and start kneading. Add the extra water, bit by bit, until the mixture comes together into a dough. Knead on a medium speed for 5 minutes, or until you have a smooth and elastic dough. Alternatively, if doing by hand, measure out the dry ingredients into a large bowl, make a well in the middle and add the 200 ml (7 fl oz/scant 1 cup) water, then mix together, adding more water if it feels too dry to come together. Tip out onto a floured surface and knead for 5–10 minutes until you have a smooth and elastic dough. Form the dough into a ball. If you press it with your finger, it should bounce back without leaving an indent. At this point, it's ready to rest.

Shape the dough into a smooth ball and grease with oil, then cover with a damp cloth and leave to rise for 1–2 hours, knocking it back about halfway through (it should roughly double in size).

Once risen, divide the dough into four pieces and fold and shape them back into smooth balls, with the seam tucked underneath. Place on a greased tray, cover loosely with oiled cling film (plastic wrap) and allow to prove for a further 15 minutes.

Once risen for a second time, roll out the dough portions into thin oblong shapes. Slash four slits in one half and divide the rosemary, goat's cheese and grapes over the other half. Fold over the slashed top, return to the greased tray and leave to prove again for 1 hour.

Preheat the oven to 220°C fan (475°F).

Remove the cling film and brush the *fougasse* with oil, then bake in the oven for 15 minutes. Serve warm.

RIB OF BEEF WITH SAUCE VIÈRGE À LA PROVENÇALE

SERVES 4

1–1.2 kg (2 lb 4 oz–2 lb 11 oz)
  rib of beef
a few sprigs of rosemary
fleur de sel and freshly ground
  black pepper

FOR THE SAUCE VIÈRGE
90 ml (3 fl oz/$\frac{1}{3}$ cup) olive oil
1 large bunch of parsley,
  leaves picked
2 garlic cloves
zest and juice of 2 unwaxed
  lemons
½ teaspoon salt
plenty of freshly ground
  black pepper

A quality rib of beef, cooked with the bone in, makes such a tasty main meal. I love roasting it on a wood-fired barbecue or oven, but a gas barbecue also works fine. The most important part is to buy the meat at a good butcher. He or she will advise you on the amount you need – remember, it looks bigger than it is, given the bone. Everyone will love the taste of this beautiful steak with layers of citrus-herbaceous sauce, and it will make a stunning Sunday special served with your favourite potatoes and salad.

If you are cooking on coal, make sure the coals are hot, grey and ready to barbecue (if you have a chimney starter, that should only take 15–20 minutes). Make sure the grill grate is also hot, so put that on 10 minutes before you start cooking.

Prepare the meat by patting it dry and rubbing it with salt and pepper, then cover and leave to get to room temperature.

Once ready, place the rib of beef on the grill. For medium, cook for 20 minutes per 450 g (1 lb); for rare, cook for 15 minutes per 450 g (1 lb), turning it over halfway through.

Meanwhile, put all the ingredients for the sauce into a bowl and blend with a hand-held blender until smooth, then check the seasoning. It should be tangy and salty to stand up to the juicy meat. Pour into a jug ready for serving.

Remove the beef and cut into it to check whether it is sufficiently cooked, or for more precision use a meat thermometer (52°C/125°F for rare, 60°C/140°F for medium and 71°C/160°F for well done). Now let it rest for a few minutes, if you have an oven that isn't full, you can leave it to rest in there for 10 minutes at 50°C/125°F. Otherwise, just leave it to rest in the kitchen in a pan with a dome lid on to conserve the heat.

Once all your guests are assembled, use a carving knife to separate the meat from the bone and cut it against the grain into slices about 2 cm (¾ in) thick. Serve on a large, warm platter and pour over the sauce.

PEACHES POACHED IN PINK GIN WITH PISTACHIO CRUMBLE AND CRÈME FRAÎCHE

SERVES 4

300 ml (10 fl oz/1¼ cups) water
100 g (3½ oz/scant ½ cup) caster
   (superfine) sugar, or to taste
sprig of rosemary or thyme
60 ml (2 fl oz/¼ cup) pink gin
4 slightly firm peaches, halved
   and stoned
crème fraîche, to serve

FOR THE PISTACHIO CRUMBLE
75 g (2½ oz/scant ⅔ cup) plain
   (all-purpose) or spelt flour,
   or as needed
75 g (2½ oz) pistachio nut
   kernels, finely crushed
50 g (1¾ oz) unsalted butter,
   softened
50 g (1¾ oz/scant ¼ cup) caster
   (superfine) sugar

Gin's pronounced herbaceous flavours make it great for cooking with. Here it makes an aromatic poaching liquid and gives this dessert an extra little kick of taste and colour.

Preheat the oven to 180°C fan (400°F) and line a baking tray (pan) with parchment paper.

First, make the pistachio crumble. Put all the ingredients into a bowl and combine with your fingers to make a crumbly texture, adding more flour if necessary. Spread the mixture out evenly on the prepared baking tray and bake in the oven for 15–20 minutes until golden. Remove from the oven and allow to cool.

Meanwhile, put the water, sugar and rosemary or thyme into a wide saucepan or deep frying pan and bring to the boil. Let it thicken until it becomes syrupy. Add the gin and reduce the heat to a gentle simmer. Place the peaches into the liquid and cook for 10–15 minutes until tender but not falling apart. Remove the peaches from the pan and set aside, then boil the liquid again for 5 minutes to reduce it further. Test for sufficient sweetness, adding sugar if you feel it's too tart.

Spoon two peaches into a bowl, add a couple of tablespoons of the syrup and a dollop of crème fraîche on top and then some of the crumble. Serve immediately.

THE HARVEST

Harvest is the emotional culmination of a busy year in the vines. It feels like an eternity to get from the long, cold days of winter and bare trunks to the first leaves sprouting and then tiny baby grapes appearing after the vine flowers in May. After that, the sun suddenly becomes stronger and it all speeds up. Great bunches of berries appear, first green, then lilac, to finish plump, deep purple and ready to be pressed for our rosé wines.

In the past, harvest dates were fixed, rather than being determined by the ripeness of the fruit. Today we worship the grape, and we observe them constantly to find out whether it's time to go out and get them into the cellar. Different varieties mature at different times, and so, luckily, the harvest is naturally staggered over a few weeks. Here at the Domaine, we usually begin with the Cinsault grapes, followed by the Vermentinos (called Rolle in Provence) and lastly the delicious Grenache Noires (see left), which take an extra dose of sun to develop their amazing peachy aromas. We mostly stick to a fast-paced harvest by machine at night to avoid the grapes oxygenating, which would produce darker rosés, with less freshness. There's a real sense of magic to being out under the stars and seeing your harvest come in during the last balmy summer nights. But the highlight we all can't wait for is our harvest lunch, which we host once we've hand-harvested the parcels that are the most delicate. A long table is set in the vineyard, under the shade of the olive trees, and we feast on sharing dishes, fresh bread and cheese, enjoying last year's rosé wine before everyone scampers for a lunchtime nap.

ROSÉ IS THE NEW PINK

BY JEANY CRONK

If you love rosé, come to Provence

There are a few reasons why Provence rosé is special. To the astonishment of many, it's said to be the oldest wine region in France, where the Greeks first planted some of their native grapes after landing near Marseille, more than 2,000 years ago. It's also the only region in the world to truly specialise in rosé. The pale and fresh rosé wines we love today were first created about half a century ago, by the innovative Ott family and the female pioneer winemaker, Régine Sumeire. They first used technology typical of elevated white winemaking to achieve the luminous rose-petal pink or pale peach colour that is the hallmark of a good Provence rosé.

How do we make rosé?

Rosé is made from red varietals, typically Grenache, Syrah and Cinsault. These are ballsy red grapes and thrive in our Mediterranean climate. The trick to not ending up with a 'nearly red' is to control how long the grape skins – which are responsible for colour and tannins – remain in contact with the juice. Very short maceration times mean only a little colour can transfer from the skins to the juice and therefore the wines will have just a touch of pink. You could also say that while we are using red grapes, the vinification method is much closer to white winemaking.

Keep it cool

Temperature is another key factor and keeping everything cool means we can extract and preserve more of the delicate aromas during the winemaking process. So, it's rather fitting that, to keep the temperatures low, the farmers in Provence have begun to harvest at night. The days during harvest time at the end of summer are still hot and harnessing the drop in temperatures after midnight is the key to making our fragrant wines.

'The goal is to find elements that will then be blended together to make a more interesting wine with different dimensions to it.'

The secret's in the blend

Another noteworthy element is that our rosés are always 'cuvées', the word for a wine that is a blend of several grape varieties. So the *assemblage* (blending) is in fact a crucial part of our job as Provence winemakers. The goal is to find elements that will then be blended together to make a more interesting wine with different dimensions to it. The process can be compared to perfume making and we similarly look for head, heart and final notes to craft a truly delicious taste experience.

How to drink a pale pink

A rosé from Provence is very aromatic and always dry, so it's the ultimate food-friendly wine. This is because we get plenty of aromas from the red grapes, but also lots of freshness and balance. Most rosés do not go through malolactic fermentation, a process that makes reds and some whites creamy, because we really want to underline the vibrant citrus and floral aromas. These wines naturally go so well with seafood, complementing the juicy salinity of fish and shellfish. But rosés also work with light meats and Mediterranean food, and they cut effortlessly through spice and love herbaceous flavours. The more high-end versions, especially if aged in oak, can match steaks and creamy cheeses, as well as caramelised fruit desserts beautifully. The general rule is: don't overthink it – pour yourself a glass, close your eyes and enjoy!

P.S. Don't overchill your rosé! You'll find the aromas open best at around 8–10°C (46–50°F) and remember that your refrigerator will be at about 5°C (41°F), so let it warm up a bit if you want to make the most of a good bottle.

MODERN PISTOU SOUP

SERVES 4

olive oil, for cooking

1 white onion, finely chopped

100 g (3½ oz) smoked bacon
    lardons, cubed

3 garlic cloves, finely chopped

150 g (5½ oz) new potatoes,
    cut into 1 cm (½ in) cubes

150 g (5½ oz) courgettes
    (zucchini), cut into 1 cm
    (½ in) cubes

3 tomatoes, cut into 1 cm
    (½ in) cubes

1 x 400 g (14 oz) tin of white
    cannellini beans, drained

750 ml (25 fl oz/3 cups)
    very good chicken stock

salt and freshly ground
    black pepper

FOR THE PISTOU

2 bunches of basil leaves (reserve
    a few for serving)

3 garlic cloves, peeled

150 ml (5 fl oz/scant ⅔ cup)
    olive oil

50 g (1¾ oz) Parmesan, grated

fleur de sel

Pistou soup tends to get a little mistreated down in Provence, its land of origin. It is rarely deemed worthy of a place on a restaurant menu and when it is, the *pistou* itself – or 'pesto' to use the Italian word more widely known across the pond – is ungenerous and the broth over-beany. But when given a little attention, it's a mighty dish that can be both elegant and completely delicious. The addition of smoked lardons gives it an undernote of smokiness that is savoury and comforting. Serve with plenty of extra *pistou*, which it is worth noting lacks the pine nuts of the Genovese variant.

While I usually preferred jarred beans, this recipe lends itself better to tinned as they will retain their shape better – or, in an ideal world, freshly podded beans (allow an extra 20 minutes cooking time if using these). Blanching the basil keeps its vibrant colour without losing the aromatics.

Heat a glug of olive oil in a saucepan over a medium heat and fry the onion and lardons for 6–7 minutes until the lardons are golden. Add the garlic and cook for 2 minutes, then go in with the potatoes, courgettes, tomatoes and beans. Bring to a simmer and cook for 10–15 minutes, or until all the vegetables are tender. Season with salt and pepper.

In the meantime, make the *pistou*. Bring a saucepan of salted water to the boil. Have a large bowl of ice and water ready. Blanch the basil leaves for 5 seconds, then fish them out with tongs and drop them straight into the iced water. Drain and pat dry (or take for a spin in a salad spinner). Add the garlic and a pinch of fleur de del to a pestle and mortar and grind to a paste, then add the basil and start bashing with 3 tablespoons of the oil. Keep adding the olive oil until you have a finely ground consistency, then add the Parmesan. Alternatively, you can use a food processor – just throw it all in together and pulse to the desired consistency.

Ladle the soup into bowls and add a spoonful of *pistou* to each bowl, finishing with a few extra basil leaves.

COQ AU VIN ROSÉ

SERVES 4

1.8 kg (4 lb) chicken
unsalted butter, for cooking
5 banana shallots, halved
6 garlic cloves, peeled
350 ml (12 fl oz/1½ cups)
    rosé wine
1 fennel bulb, thinly sliced
    (on a mandoline if possible)
2 unwaxed lemons, thinly sliced
    (on a mandoline if possible)
olive oil, for brushing
1 bunch of radishes, trimmed
salt and freshly ground black
    pepper
boiled potatoes or baguette,
    to serve

This lighter and brighter summer spin on the comfort food classic is lemony and vibrant, and couldn't be simpler to make. Salting the chicken ahead is worth the additional step, even if it's just for an hour or two (but it can be done a couple of days in advance). The salt penetrates the chicken, seasoning it to perfection while also helping the skin get extra crispy.

Generously rub salt all over the chicken – you should use about 2 teaspoons of salt. Set aside until ready to cook. At this point you can leave the chicken covered in the fridge for a day or set aside at room temperature while the oven preheats.

Preheat the oven to 220°C fan (475°F).

Melt a knob of butter in a large heavy-based saucepan or casserole dish (Dutch oven) over a medium heat (I use a wide cast-iron pan for the job). Add the shallots and cook for 5–6 minutes until they start to colour nicely, then add the garlic and cook for 2 minutes. Add the chicken, breast-side up, and cook for 4–6 minutes until the base of the chicken begins to colour and crisp. Pour in the rosé and simmer for 2 minutes.

Lift up the chicken with some tongs and slide the sliced fennel and lemons underneath. Drizzle or brush the top of the chicken with oil and place in the oven. Roast for 25 minutes, then add the radishes. Return to the oven and cook for a further 20–30 minutes, or until golden on top and the juices run clear (pull the drumstick away from the breast to check).

Serve the chicken on a platter on a bed of the lemons, fennel and radishes. Season with black pepper and serve with potatoes or lots of baguette for soaking up the juices.

HONEY-GLAZED LEEKS WITH A SAVOURY CRUMBLE

**SERVES 4
AS A SIDE DISH**

8 leeks, topped and tailed
olive oil, for drizzling
2 garlic cloves, chopped
1 tablespoon clear honey
a few sprigs of thyme
2–3 pinches of salt

FOR THE CRUMBLE
175 g (6 oz/scant 1¼ cups)
   wholemeal (whole-wheat)
   or spelt flour
90 g (3¼ oz) unsalted butter
1 teaspoon salt
100 g (3½ oz) Parmesan, grated
freshly ground black pepper

Leeks used to be my least-favourite vegetable – in fact, I remember as a child sitting in front of them for hours, refusing to eat them. Well, times have changed, and I love them now. What makes them delicious is baking them until they are caramelised, and I like eating them as part of a gratin, quiche or, as I suggest here, with a crunchy savoury crumble.

Preheat the oven to 180°C fan (400°F) and line a baking tray (pan) with parchment paper.

First, make the crumble mix by combining the flour, butter and salt in a bowl with a generous pinch of pepper. I tend to do the mixing by hand, but if you have a dough hook attachment on your stand mixer or an electric whisk you can use that, just take care not to overprocess. Otherwise, use your fingers to rub the butter and flour together until you have a crumbly mixture, adding a bit more flour if it looks too greasy. Pour it onto the prepared baking tray and spread out evenly.

Put the leeks onto a large baking tray, drizzle with olive oil, then add the garlic, honey, thyme leaves (remove the stalks) and 2–3 pinches of salt, and turn them all well to ensure everything is evenly coated.

Put the leeks and the crumble into the oven at the same time, positioning the leeks in the shelf above the crumble. Bake for 35–40 minutes, until the leeks are very soft and caramelised and the crumble is evenly brown. Remove both from the oven and pour the crumble over the leeks, then add the Parmesan over the top. Return to the oven until the top is brown and crisp, about 10–15 minutes (you can also use the grill/broiler for this).

Serve as part of a meat dish or with a nice green salad if you want to keep it vegetarian.

POTATO, BLACK OLIVE AND GARLIC GRATIN

**SERVES 4
AS A SIDE DISH**

8 medium all-purpose potatoes,
    such as Agatha, Maris Piper
    or King Edward
4 garlic cloves
a few gratings of nutmeg
herbes de Provence, to taste
1–1½ tablespoons salt and freshly
    ground black pepper
unsalted butter, for greasing
150 g (5½ oz/1¼ cups) pitted
    black olives à la grecque,
    roughly chopped
600 ml (20 fl oz/2½ cups) single
    (light) cream
70 g (2½ oz) Comté, grated

Is there anything more comforting than a good potato gratin? Well, this one's even better thanks to its Provençal touch. Whenever we have a bigger meal at the Domaine, we serve one of these and there are never any leftovers. The secret here is the slow cooking, which means the potatoes melt in the mouth and are never watery.

Preheat the oven to 150°C fan (350°F).

Peel the potatoes, slice them thinly and evenly, then add them to a bowl of salted water to stop them from discolouring while you build the gratin.

Chop 3½ of the garlic cloves, keeping one half whole.

Mix together the salt, pepper, nutmeg and herbes de Provence so you can easily and quickly season each layer.

Grease a large, deep baking dish, then rub the halved garlic clove all over the bottom and sides. Add a couple of layers of potatoes to the bottom, sprinkle over some of the seasoning mix and add some of the chopped olives and garlic – try to do this as evenly as possible, taking care not to over-season. Pour over a quarter of the cream. Repeat until you have run out of potatoes, ensuring that everything is well covered with liquid (if need be, add some milk to stretch the cream). Sprinkle the cheese over the top, then finish with some seasoning mix, garlic and olives.

Cook in the oven for about 1½ hours, or until melt-in-the-mouth tender. Switch the oven to grill (broiler) and bake for a few minutes (set yourself an alarm so you don't forget) to crisp up the cheese. Serve piping hot in the dish on a wooden board.

Note
If you are in a real rush, you can parboil the potatoes (which will reduce your baking time to around 35 minutes) and it will still be very moreish!

KAKI CHUTNEY FOR
A CHEESEBOARD

4 ripe kakis (persimmons)

1 tablespoon olive oil

2 onions, finely chopped

3 tablespoons sherry or white
    wine vinegar

3 sprigs of rosemary

¼ teaspoon ground ginger

1–2 tablespoons caster
    (superfine) sugar (optional)

salt and freshly ground
    black pepper

I'd always had kaki (or persimmons) pinned as a tropical fruit, shipped in from some far-flung place … until I found them growing at the end of the track, a few metres from our home! Pomegranates too, often seen dangling from trees in our gardens, serve as a happy reminder that we are in more exotic climes down here in Le Sud.

The French don't do cheese and chutney. But that's not to say we can't, and this goes remarkably well with brie and Roquefort, so traditions are there to be broken. Just be sure to serve the cheese course after the main…

Cut the kakis in half and scoop out the flesh with a spoon. Set aside.

Heat the oil in a saucepan over a low heat and cook the onion slowly for 10 minutes (cover with a lid if it starts to dry out at all).

Add the sherry or white wine vinegar, then add the kaki flesh and the rosemary sprigs. Season with salt, pepper and the ground ginger.

Continue cooking for a further 10 minutes over a low heat, just long enough for the mixture to soften. Taste at this point, and add 1–2 tablespoons of caster sugar if it's tasting too sour. Remove from the heat and leave to cool.

Serve with a beautiful selection of French cheeses. Decant into a sterilised jar (see Fig Jam recipe on page 145). Refrigerate after use, then it can be kept for up to 2 months.

DARK CHOCOLATE FONDANT WITH FLEUR DE SEL AND THYME-INFUSED WHIPPED CREAM

SERVES 6–8

FOR THE CHOCOLATE CAKE

200 g (7 oz) good-quality dark
cooking chocolate

150 g (5½ oz) unsalted butter

6 eggs

50 g (1¾ oz/scant ½ cup)
cornflour (cornstarch)

150 g (5½ oz/²⁄₃ cup) caster
(superfine) sugar

1 teaspoon fleur de sel

FOR THE WHIPPED CREAM

250 ml (8½ fl oz/1 cup)
whipping cream

5 sprigs of fresh thyme, plus an
extra sprig to serve

1 tablespoon mascarpone

1 tablespoon icing (powdered)
sugar

Who doesn't love a chocolate fondant cake? Fondant means 'melted' in French and to be perfect it needs to be still gooey in the centre. The salt and the thyme make for a very nice contrast to the rich chocolate and bring a touch of Provence to this popular dessert.

If you can, infuse the whipped cream the day before, or leave it at least for a few hours. Place the whipping cream in a bowl and add the thyme sprigs. Cover with cling film (plastic wrap) and keep in the refrigerator.

Just before serving, strain the cream into a mixing bowl to remove the thyme and add the mascarpone and icing sugar. Using an electric whisk, whip the cream until stiff peaks form. Be careful not to overwhip it or it will turn into butter. Store in the refrigerator until ready to use.

Preheat the oven to 180°C fan (400°F) and line a 20 cm (8 in) round cake tin (pan) with parchment paper.

In a saucepan over a very low heat, melt the chocolate and butter.

In a large mixing bowl, whisk together the eggs, cornflour and sugar. Add in the chocolate mixture and mix until homogeneous. Add the fleur de sel and stir gently.

Pour the batter into the prepared cake tin and bake for 30 minutes.

Let the cake cool for 20 minutes before transferring it to a serving plate. Serve with a dollop of cold whipped cream and decorated with the leaves of the last sprig of thyme.

PURPLE PLEASURES

THE SEASON FOR FIGS

There is more than one harvest at our Domaine. The gigantic fig tree outside La Bastide ripens at the same time as the first grapes these days, towards the end of August. It provides us with a month's worth of ripe, deep purple, fragrant figs. It's brilliant to be able to pick your own dessert or cheese board accompaniment, and we love to fill our baskets first thing in the morning.

Figs are a big part of Provençal cuisine – 75 per cent of France's figs are harvested down the road in the Gapeau Valley, and they are considered a real delicacy by the best pâtissiers. If you are in the region at the right time, you can buy them aplenty in most shops and markets to snack on and add them to a myriad of sweet and savoury recipes. You can also preserve them by cooking them gently and then use as a condiment for cheese or for spooning over fromage frais with some thyme flowers for a tasty dessert.

The leaves of the fig tree are delicately fragranced and make a lovely scented simple syrup for a fig cocktail or to drizzle over melon with finely sliced ham. If you heat some shredded leaves with olive oil (take them out after 10 minutes or so), you can make a scented oil that works beautifully drizzled over white fish or vanilla ice cream.

FIG GIN SPRITZ

ice

50 ml (1¾ fl oz/3 tablespoons)
    dry gin

25 ml (¾ fl oz/1½ tablespoons)
    fig syrup (see below), or more
    to taste

75 ml (2½ fl oz/5 tablespoons)
    sparkling wine

sparkling water, to top

½ fig, to decorate

FOR THE FIG SYRUP

100 ml (3½ fl oz/scant ½ cup)
    water

100 g (3½ oz/scant ½ cup) caster
    (superfine) sugar

1–2 fig leaves, torn

The delicate, sweet scent when you walk past a fig tree is so pretty and you can easily capture it by making a syrup from the leaves. This is lovely over vanilla ice cream or some fresh goat's cheese curd, but it also works very well as a fragrant drinks ingredient. The perfect cocktail to clink glasses with on a beautiful summer evening, with the heady scent of fig. You can purchase dried fig leaves easily online if you don't happen to live near a fig tree.

First, make the fig syrup. Put the water and sugar into a saucepan over a medium heat and simmer until the sugar dissolves and the syrup thickens. Add the fig leaves and continue to simmer over a very low heat for 15 minutes, then pour through a sieve (fine mesh strainer) into a bottle or jar and allow to cool. This makes more than you need, but leftovers can be stored in the refrigerator for up to 2 weeks.

Next, make the cocktail. You can prepare this in a jug (pitcher) or in a shaker. Half-fill the shaker with ice, then add the double measure of gin and the fig syrup, or a little more if you prefer a sweeter version. Give a shake, or a stir if you are using a jug. Add some more ice to a large wine glass or tumbler and pour in the mixture from the shaker. Add the sparkling wine and then top up with sparkling water. You can inverse the proportions of sparkling wine and water for a lighter version, or even just add sparkling water if you want something non-alcoholic. Garnish with half a fig. For a naughtier version, you can soak the fig in some gin beforehand.

BRULÉED FIGS WITH BEETROOT, ENDIVE AND WALNUT-PARSLEY PISTOU

SERVES 4

8 figs

2 tablespoons caster (superfine) sugar

3 cooked beetroots (beets)

1½ tablespoons red wine vinegar

salt

2 heads of endive, or other robust salad leaf

100 g (3½ oz) crumbly blue cheese

FOR THE WALNUT-PARSLEY PISTOU

60 g (2 oz) walnut halves

20 g (¾ oz) flat-leaf parsley, leaves picked

100 ml (3½ fl oz/scant ½ cup) extra virgin olive oil, plus extra for drizzling

½ garlic clove, peeled

pinch of salt

50 g (1¾ oz) Parmesan, grated

This late-summer, early autumn (fall) salad is an excellent way to showcase the bounty of fresh figs weighing down the local fig trees around harvest time. Glazing the figs with a little sugar before torching them gives them a glossy, crisp, sugary shell, which pairs perfectly with the salty, rich blue cheese. If you don't have a kitchen blowtorch, place them under a very hot grill (broiler) until caramelised.

Preheat the oven to 160°C fan (350°F).

First, make the pistou. Place the walnut halves on a baking sheet and toast in the oven for 5 minutes, or until they are lightly coloured and aromatic. Set aside to cool.

Chop the parsley finely and add to a small bowl along with the extra virgin olive oil. In a pestle and mortar or a small food processor, crush or pulse the cooled walnuts with the garlic, salt and Parmesan until roughly ground but still a bit chunky. Add to the parsley oil and stir to combine. Drizzle with a little more oil to cover, then set aside.

Cut the figs in half, stem to base. Place them on a baking sheet, and sprinkle their flesh with half of the sugar. Torch them with a kitchen blowtorch until the sugar melts, or place under a hot grill (broiler). Wait a minute or two, then scatter with the remaining sugar and repeat until the sugar is melted and has formed a crisp, caramel sheen.

Cut the beetroot into small chunks, place in a large bowl and toss with the red wine vinegar and the salt. Add the endive, or other leaves, and toss to coat. Divide the beetroot and leaves between plates, add the fig halves, spoon over the pistou and finish with the crumbled blue cheese.

PROVENÇAL FIG JAM

40 g (1½ oz) of shelled walnuts,
  crushed
2 sprigs of thyme
250 g (9 oz) of purple figs
135 g (4½ oz/scant ²/₃ cup)
  caster (superfine) of sugar
1 tablespoon olive oil
juice of 1 small lemon

Fig jam was one of the first gifts we received from locals when we arrived in Provence in the autumn (fall) of 2009, so it holds a special place in our hearts. It's a great condiment to eat with cheeses and cold meats, or ice cream and *fromage blanc*. I like to add some roasted walnuts and fresh thyme to give it some extra texture and herbaceous aromas to complement the natural sweetness of the figs. If you happen to have a lot of figs, go large and make some friends and family happy with a homemade gift.

Preheat the oven to 140°C fan (325°F) and place a 500 ml (1 lb 2 oz) jar and lid inside for 10 minutes to sterilise them.

In a frying pan (skillet) over a medium-high heat, dry roast the walnuts. Add the thyme leaves by running down the sprig with your fingers and discard the stalks. Turn frequently for about 3 minutes to ensure nothing burns. Remove from the heat and leave to cool.

Clean the figs by slicing off the tops and bottoms, then quarter them.

Heat the olive oil in a medium saucepan over a medium heat, then add the figs, walnuts, thyme and sugar. Cook gently for 15 minutes, partially covered, until you get a nice, thick consistency, then add the lemon juice. Turn frequently and keep an eye on the temperature to ensure nothing burns.

Pour the jam into your sterilised jar, seal and turn it upside down. Leave it standing on its lid for a few minutes, then leave it to cool down.

The jam will keep for up to 2 years if stored in a cool, dry place. Refrigerate once opened.

THE COAST

LA CÔTE

~

THE RIVIERA LIFE

Not many places can match the French Mediterranean coast for glamour and sheer natural beauty. It's a place where people from all over the world come together, feet in the sand, looking out to the glittering sea, immersed in the moment.

The salty scent of the Mediterranean tickling your nose, umbrella pines giving generous shade to fine sandy beaches and flags flapping in the breeze give an intense feeling of freedom. It's an easy voyage back in time to the days when Brigitte Bardot strolled down by the old port of Saint-Tropez barefoot, setting this small fishing village alight with paparazzi flashbulbs, with her unique bohemian appeal. But it was not just she who fell for the lightness of being on the French coast: Picasso is said to have sold one of his still life paintings to buy a house near Cannes, while Colette and Françoise Sagan came to Saint-Tropez to write. Matisse and Chagall paid tribute to the unique quality of the light, and both painted passionately by the coast. In fact, Matisse spent nearly 30 years in the region, and some of his most famous works were created here, including *La Danse*, and his painting *Luxe, Calme et Volupté* (luxury, calm and voluptuousness), was inspired by his love for the Riviera.

The Côte d'Azur, so named because of its vibrant blue sky and sea, stretches from Menton, near the Italian border, to well behind the vast beaches of Saint-Tropez. There are many towns and villages lining this iconic route, La Nationale 7, which was the traditional coastal road taken by French families to their summer holidays, as well as by the world's most famous stars in their convertibles. You'll find a huge variety of destinations here, ranging from the bustling vibes of its biggest town, Nice, to small harbour villages such as Théoule-sur-Mer and, of course, the celebrated locations of Saint-Tropez and Antibes. What they have in common is a focus on eating seafood alfresco and huge terraces with parasols lining the seafront. The houses are often rendered in vibrant colours, adding to the visual feel-good factor, and fragrant climbing jasmine or a shocking-pink bougainvillaea bring an extra touch to many facades. Palms and citrus trees grow well in this milder climate, so you will see both in abundance, often with plentiful fruit still ripening. The famous Promenade de la Croisette in Cannes is lined with magnificent palm trees and many types of *palmier* lend their prettily structured leaves to gardens and courtyards.

A STROLL THROUGH SAINT-TROPEZ

Still the most iconic location on the coast, this former fishing village is the epitome of relaxed glamour, and while luxury boutiques have sprung up in many of its shaded side streets, it has managed to keep most of its aura of simplicity and prettiness. There are also some iconic addresses that have not changed much over the years, which provide continuity to this village affectionately named 'St Trop'.

Saint-Tropez is full of picturesque corners, like a perfect fan of pink and peach colours, pretty doorways, awnings and vintage vespas. Stroll through the old town to discover the prettiest spots, and an incredible view from the old citadel fortress that overlooks the village. The legendary Hotel La Ponche, just above the harbour, is where Brigitte Bardot and her co-stars took their aperitifs on the small, protected terrace, with the view of the glittering Mediterranean and boats gently gliding past. From there, you can easily access the Sentier du Littoral, a small footpath that starts just below Saint-Tropez's

citadel that takes you all the way to the next bay with the beautiful Canebiers and Salins beaches. It is a perfect way to explore the coastline, especially when it's not too hot.

If you don't fancy the walk, take a seat right in the middle of the town on the tiny pebble beach La Glaye, with a coffee and snack in hand. You can already glimpse the bright blue sea from the mayoral square above, through a pink archway. This charming village beach is captured today in millions of Instagram pictures – it's especially lovely early in the morning if you can make it there.

ORANGE FLOWER AND ALMOND SABLE BISCUITS

MAKES 20 BISCUITS

1 large egg
100 g (3½ oz/½ cup) light brown
 soft sugar
90 g (3¼ oz) unsalted butter,
 softened
1 teaspoon orange blossom water
zest of 1 orange
100 g (3½ oz/generous ¾ cup)
 cake and pastry flour, plus extra
 for dusting
130 g (4½ oz/1¼ cups) ground
 almonds (almond meal)

Orange flower is a typical smell of the South of France and it is often used in patisserie, such as brioche or madeleines. I find it works well with almonds, like in these crumbly, buttery biscuits (cookies), which are lovely with a creamy coffee.

Whisk the egg in a bowl, then add the sugar and whisk again until creamy. Add the softened butter and whisk until you have a buttercream. Add the orange blossom water and orange zest and stir in.

Next, fold in the flour and ground almonds, integrating it with your fingers until homogeneous and no longer sticky, feeling soft and silky to the touch. If the dough is too wet, add a little extra flour. Form into a ball, then place in a bowl, cover and rest in the refrigerator for at least 30 minutes.

Preheat the oven to 170°C fan (375°F) and line a baking sheet with parchment paper.

Once rested, cut the dough in half and roll out on a cool, floured surface. Personally, I prefer them a bit smaller and thicker, I'd say about 7 mm (¼ in) thick. I use a shot glass to cut them out, but if you have a pastry cutter, flour a small one and use that. Place the finished biscuits on the prepared baking sheet, leaving a bit of space between them. If you need to bake in batches, return the dough you are not using to the refrigerator.

Bake the biscuits in the oven for about 15 minutes until light brown around the edges but still a little squidgy in the middle – take care not to overbake them as they will dry out. Once baked, remove from the oven and allow to cool on the sheet before lifting them off to cool completely on a wire rack. Store in a lined tin or glass jar. They are great as a snack, but also lovely with a chocolate-based dessert, or to dunk in your café au lait.

CATCH OF THE DAY

The daily fish market in Saint-Tropez is in a covered alleyway, just past the famous red awnings of the Café Senéquier, and has a beautifully presented selection of seafood. It's a real treat to shop there and you are certain to find everything you need for a classic *bouillabaisse*, properly prepared fillets or a fish that you can grill whole on the barbecue, with some fresh *garrigue* herbs thrown on the fire.

There are only a small handful of merchants and, excitingly, there is a fresh catch (*l'arrivage du jour*) from the surrounding area as well as a much more extensive selection from further afield.

There are sea bream (*dorades*) from the Toulon area, local red mullet, fresh squid and occasionally even tuna from Marseilles. As you exit the fish market, you'll see the bar Chez Madeleine, a local institution where you can eat a dozen fresh oysters or some langoustines, washed down with a cool Vermentino from one of the local vineyards. There is always a fun crowd and laughter in the air, so I encourage you to drop in and stay awhile, people-watching.

SAINT-TROPEZ CEVICHE

SERVES 4

300 g (10½ oz) very fresh
   boneless bass, bream or small
   red mullet fillet
coarse salt, for curing the fish
½ red onion, thinly sliced
1 tablespoon red wine vinegar
1½ teaspoons caster
   (superfine) sugar
juice of 3 limes
½ teaspoon Espelette pepper,
   plus extra to serve
pinch of salt
1 small grapefruit or orange,
   segmented
½ fennel bulb, very thinly shaved
   on a mandoline
5 radishes or ½ watermelon
   radish (if available),
   very thinly sliced
handful of coriander (cilantro)
   leaves or fennel fronds
extra virgin olive oil, for drizzling

The perfect dish to make the most of very fresh fish, this is also a nod to the summer months, when we're inspired by the more eclectic fare that's come to the Riviera with international visitors. A gorgeous, clean and light dish with vibrant colours, it's the kind of no-cook classic you crave in the sun-scorched summer months.

Pat the fish dry and place it on a non-reactive dish or tray. Season liberally with coarse salt and refrigerate for about 20 minutes.

Meanwhile, put the red onion into a bowl with the vinegar and ½ teaspoon of the sugar. Toss well to coat and set aside to pickle.

In a separate bowl, combine the lime juice with the remaining sugar, Espelette pepper and pinch of salt.

Once lightly cured, brush the excess salt off the fish and slice it thinly, as you would sashimi, then submerge it in the lime juice mixture. Cover and set aside in the refrigerator for 30 minutes.

After 30 minutes, toss the grapefruit and fennel through the lime juice and fish to dress it. Remove from the juices and arrange on a plate, then add the radishes, pickled onion and the coriander leaves (or fennel fronds). Drizzle with extra virgin olive oil (this is the Mediterranean after all!) and sprinkle with a little more Espelette pepper.

BOUILLABAISSE FOR BUSY PEOPLE

SERVES 4

250 g (9 oz) large shell-on raw
   prawns (shrimp)
4 small red mullet, cleaned
750 ml (25 fl oz/3 cups)
   cold water
olive oil, for cooking
1 onion, diced
½ fennel bulb, diced (keep the
   fronds for garnishing)
pinch of salt
3 garlic cloves, chopped
1 good pinch of saffron threads
   or spigol spice mix
4 large ripe tomatoes,
   roughly chopped
500 g (1 lb 2 oz) mussels,
   scrubbed
croutons, to serve

FOR THE SUN-DRIED
TOMATO ROUILLE
25 g (1 oz) soft white bread
75 ml (2½ fl oz/5 tablespoons)
   hot fish stock
8 sun-dried tomatoes
1 garlic clove, crushed
1–2 tablespoons extra virgin
   olive oil
Espelette pepper, to taste
salt, to taste

Some might consider it sacrilege to mess with what is considered one of the great fish stews, but if the lengthy cook time of this Marseille dish has ever stood in the way of you making it, this one is for you. Traditionally it's a half-day job, but I've taken some cheat steps to take this from 'project cook' to 'weekday dinner party' while not compromising on flavour.

When you buy your fish, ask your fishmonger to fillet it but keep the bones as these will form the basis of your stock.

Peel the prawns and put the heads and shells into a saucepan. Fillet the mullet – if your fishmonger hasn't done it for you – and add the bones and trimmings to the pan with the prawn heads. Cover with the water. Put the peeled prawns and mullet fillets back in the refrigerator, covered, until needed. Bring the stock to a simmer over a low heat and cook for 45 minutes.

While the fish stock is simmering, grab another pan and drizzle the base with olive oil. Heat over a medium-low heat, then add the onion, fennel and a pinch of salt and sweat for 8 minutes. Add the garlic and cook for a further 2 minutes until it starts to colour.

When the stock is ready, strain it through a fine-mesh sieve (strainer) into a bowl. Repeat if there are still a few remaining bits.

Pour the stock into the pan with the onions and fennel and add the saffron and tomatoes. Bring to a simmer and cook for 10 minutes.

Meanwhile, make the rouille. Put the bread, hot stock, tomatoes, garlic and 1 tablespoon of the olive oil into a food processor and blend until rich and velvety, adding more oil if needed. Season to taste with Espelette pepper and salt, then set aside.

Transfer the soup to a blender and blend until very smooth, then return to the pan, bring to a simmer and add the mussels and prawns. Cook for 2–3 minutes, then add the mullet fillets (which can be more fragile and take less time). Once the mussels are open and cooked, divide the soup between bowls, making sure everyone gets a little of each element. Serve with croutons topped with the rouille to dip in the soup.

COD AND SOCCA CROQUETTES WITH DILL AND LEMON SAUCE

SERVES 4

FOR THE CROQUETTES

2 tablespoons sunflower oil, plus extra for cooking

2 large cod fillets (approx. 280–300 g /10–10½ oz)

200 g (7 oz) tinned chickpeas (garbanzos), drained

150 g (½ oz/1⅓ cups) chickpea (gram) flour, plus extra for dusting

2 tablespoons olive oil

3 medium eggs

freshly grated nutmeg, to taste

salt and freshly ground black pepper

FOR THE SAUCE

2 medium egg yolks

170 ml (5¾ fl oz/¾ cup) light olive oil or sunflower oil

zest and juice of 1 unwaxed lemon

1 bunch of dill, finely chopped

salt and freshly ground black pepper

Socca is a flatbread that is the staple snack of Nice. You will see stands with small wood-fired ovens making it at most markets. The flour used is made from milled chickpeas (garbanzos), so the bonus is the extra protein and goodness. You can buy chickpea (gram) flour in most wholefood shops, but here you can buy it in most supermarkets too. If you don't want to make fresh mayonnaise, a good-quality shop-bought one will do the trick and save time.

Preheat the oven to 160°C fan (350°F).

Heat a little oil in a frying pan (skillet) over a medium–high heat and cook the cod for 2 minutes on each side, until barely opaque. Transfer to a bowl, add the chickpeas, 100 g (3½ oz/scant 1 cup) of the chickpea flour and the olive oil. Beat two of the eggs and add to the bowl. Season well with salt, pepper and nutmeg, then use a fork to mix everything to a paste, adding a little more chickpea flour if it's too runny.

Put the remaining chickpea flour onto a plate and beat the remaining egg on a second plate. Pour the 2 tablespoons of sunflower oil into a non-stick frying pan over a medium-high heat – make sure the oil does not burn or smoke.

Coat your hands in some flour, then form the cod mixture into small round croquettes – they are meant to be finger-food size. Roll the croquettes in the egg and then roll them in the chickpea flour.

Once you finish the croquettes, add them to the pan and cook for about 2 minutes on each side until browned – you may have to turn up the heat a little, but make sure they don't burn. Once they have crisped up, place them on a baking tray (pan) and bake in the oven for 15 minutes.

While they are baking, make the sauce. Beat the eggs in a food processor or with an electric whisk, then slowly pour in the oil, making sure the yolks have fully absorbed the oil before pouring in more. Once it has a nice unctuous consistency, add the lemon zest, juice and dill. Season with salt and pepper and whisk gently to combine. Transfer to a bowl.

Remove the croquettes from the oven and arrange on a platter alongside the bowl of sauce.

ROASTED BABY GEM LETTUCE WITH KING PRAWNS AND PISTACHIO PESTO

SERVES 4

16 raw king prawns (jumbo shrimp), shells on and defrosted if frozen

2 baby gem lettuces

3 tablespoons 50/50 olive and sunflower oil, for frying

FOR THE PISTACHIO PESTO

50 g (1¾ oz) of shelled unsalted pistachios

zest and juice of 1 unwaxed lemon

100 ml (3½ fl oz/scant ½ cup) extra virgin olive oil

1 garlic clove, peeled

small handful of basil leaves, washed

¼ teaspoon red chilli paste

½ teaspoon fleur de sel, plus extra to serve

pinch of white pepper

A fresh, yet rich and smoky dish, which perfectly complements juicy prawns (shrimp). Pistachios were planted widely in Provence before the 20th century and used in desserts. There is a revival of Pistachio planting in Provence and I know of several, experimental orchards locally. The plant would be great as a complement to viticulture, as it's a hardy bush that thrives on plenty of sunshine. Pistachios only produce fruit every other year and, unlike vines, need pollinators to produce it, so healthy insect populations are essential.

First, make the pesto. Add the pistachios to a small food processor or into a bowl if using a hand blender. Add the lemon zest and juice, olive oil, garlic, basil, chilli, salt and pepper. Blend to a coarse paste. Check the seasoning, it should be salty enough to season the salad and the prawns. Set aside.

Wash and dry the lettuce, then cut in half. Heat a griddle pan over a high heat and coat with a tablespoon of the olive oil and sunflower oil mixture. Place the lettuces on the griddle, cut-sides down and grill until slightly charred, and the griddle marks are visible on the lettuces – no need to turn them. Remove from the pan and set them on a platter (or one per plate if you are serving this as a starter).

Heat the remaining oil in a frying pan (skillet) over a high heat. Add the shell-on prawns and fry for 2 minutes on each side. Remove from the heat and leave to cool in the pan.

When cool enough to handle, remove and discard the heads and shells from the prawns. Return the prawns to the pan and set over a gentle heat. Add half of the pesto to the pan and warm through for a minute or two, turning the prawns until evenly coated in the pesto.

Place the prawns neatly next to the charred lettuce halves and drizzle over the remaining pesto. Add a pinch of fleur de sel for some extra taste and crunch. Serve with some roasted sourdough crostini to mop up the pesto or alternatively add some fresh linguine to the pan with the prawns for a more substantial meal (if doing the latter option, you may wish to increase the pesto quantity by a third).

WHEN IN SAINT-TROPEZ

Saint-Tropez has its very own cake, the *tarte Tropézienne*, made famous by Brigitte Bardot, who loved this giant brioche filled with crème pâtissière and covered with big crystals of crunchy sugar. The original bakery of this comfort food is on the famous Place des Lices, the main square, which is home to the weekly markets, cafés and boules competitions. There are numerous versions of this cake, sometimes with additional fruit fillings, or orange flower or lemon aromas, but in my opinion the original, with vanilla-flavoured crème pâtissière, is the best! It's an indulgent dessert, but also a lovely midday or afternoon snack that's perfect with a good coffee. Better not to count calories when you indulge in this one … just enjoy the moment. You are on the gorgeous Côte d'Azur, after all.

FEET IN THE SAND

Beach clubs are always a great way to eat near the water and we refer to it as 'eating with our feet in the sand'. Many also feature comfy sun loungers with an umbrella to shade you, a perfect spot to have a rest after lunch or head out for a refreshing swim. They come in lots of different iterations, from very fancy to rustic beach shacks, but most are easygoing and family friendly. We often head to a beach club as a treat when we have visitors to enjoy the relaxed vibe and the beautiful view. A particularly nice seafront location to visit is the Lily of the Valley Hotel in La Croix-Valmer. Their restaurant, La Brigantine, is beautifully styled and serves fresh and aromatic cuisine, with a strong nod to Provence's Italian links. Their talented chef Vincent Maillard has shared the following two recipes with us, which we are delighted to include here.

BAKED PROVENÇAL SPELT RISOTTO WITH SPRING VEGETABLES AND BROUSSE

SERVES 4

80 ml (2¾ fl oz/⅓ cup) olive oil

1 onion, finely chopped

100 ml (3½ fl oz/scant ½ cup)
   white wine

200 g (7 oz) pearled spelt,
   soaked overnight

2 litres (70 fl oz/8 cups)
   vegetable stock

a few sprigs of marjoram (a pinch
   if dried)

1 bunch of nasturtium flowers
   (optional, or could be replaced
   with rocket/arugula salad
   or cress)

½ head of broccoli, cut into
   small florets

8 asparagus stems

200 g (7 oz/1½ cups) petit pois,
   fresh or frozen

Sugar snap peas

60 g (2 oz) Parmesan, grated

100 g (3½ oz) brousse (or ricotta)

salt and freshly ground
   black pepper

This fresh spelt risotto recipe created by Vincent Maillard is served at La Brigantine restaurant and is a great dish to be enjoyed on a warm summer's day. The inclusion of brousse, a fresh whey cheese from Provence and Corsica, with a lovely delicate flavour, is a very nice complement to the crunchy spring vegetables, herbs and edible flowers.

Preheat the oven to 160°C fan (350°F).

Heat a tablespoon of the olive oil in a casserole dish (Dutch oven) over a medium heat and fry the onion until transparent, then deglaze with the white wine. Add the spelt and stir to coat, then add half of the stock. Cover with the lid and transfer to the oven to cook for 1½ hours, checking occasionally to ensure there is enough stock and that the spelt is not overcooked – it should retain some bite.

Meanwhile, crush the marjoram and some of the edible flowers with 2 tablespoons of the olive oil in a pestle and mortar to make a paste.

Bring a saucepan of salted water to the boil and blanch the broccoli, asparagus, sugar snap peas and petit pois for 5 minutes. Drain, then plunge them into a bowl of ice-cold water to preserve their crunch and colour. Drain again, place in a bowl and coat them with the marjoram paste.

Remove the spelt from the oven once soft, then add the remaining olive oil and Parmesan and stir until it's nice and creamy. Ensure the spelt is still warm (reheat gently if necessary), then divide between deep, warmed plates.

Add the vegetables over the top and finish with some spoonfuls of the brousse (or ricotta). Adjust the seasoning, garnish with the remaining edible flowers and serve.

STRAWBERRIES IN THEIR JUS, HONEY CREAM, CHANTILLY AND SORREL PESTO

SERVES 4

500 g (1lb 2 oz) of strawberries, washed, topped and tailed, then halved

FOR THE HONEY CREAM
1 leaf of gelatine
2 tablespoons wildflower honey
1 medium egg yolk
2½ tablespoons double (heavy) cream

FOR THE WHIPPED CREAM
50 g (2 oz) wildflower honey
200 ml (7 fl oz/scant 1 cup) whipping cream
4 medium egg yolks

FOR THE SORREL PESTO
40 g (1½ oz) sorrel leaves (can use basil as an alternative)
juice of ½ lemon
20 g (¾ oz) of almond butter
1½ tablespoons extra virgin olive oil
½ teaspoon icing (powdered) sugar

FOR THE STRAWBERRY JUS
100 g (3½ oz/scant ½ cup) caster (superfine) sugar
100 ml (3½ fl oz/scant ½ cup) filtered water
150 g (5½ oz) strawberries, washed, topped and tailed

A simplified version of a Lily of the Valley Hotel classic, this recipe is full of the gorgeous flavours of ripe strawberries, offset with the fine tartness of sorrel. The rich sweetness of wildflower honey adds a delicious touch. You can make most of it in advance, put it in the fridge and serve when you are ready.

Start with the honey cream – it needs at least 3 hours in the refrigerator before serving. Place the gelatine leaf in a small bowl of cold water and set aside to soften. Meanwhile, measure out the honey into a heatproof glass and warm gently inside a larger cup filled with hot water to ensure it liquefies. Combine the egg yolk, honey and cream in a small saucepan and gently heat until it reaches 84°C (183°F) on a sugar thermometer. Add the softened gelatine leaf and stir until everything is well combined. Remove from the heat, pour into a Tupperware with a lid and refrigerate.

Next, make the whipped cream. Liquefy the honey as in the previous step. Place the cream in a large mixing bowl, followed by the egg yolks and honey. Use a hand-held blender to whip to stiff peaks, then cover and refrigerate.

Next, make the sorrel pesto. Add all the ingredients for the pesto to a small food processor or blender, and blend to a smooth paste. Pour into a small jug, cover and refrigerate.

Thirty minutes before you want to serve, put four dessert bowls into the refrigerator to chill.

For the strawberry jus, combine the sugar and water in a medium saucepan and dissolve over a medium heat. Add the strawberries, reduce the heat to low and leave to infuse for 30 minutes. Strain through a sieve (fine mesh strainer) set over a bowl – let it drain for a few minutes.

To serve, divide the halved strawberries equally among the chilled bowls and pour over the jus. Add a spoonful of the honey cream alongside and spoon dollops of the whipped cream over the strawberries. Finish by drizzling some sorrel pesto over it all.

EATING ALFRESCO BY THE SEA

~

BY FRANKIE UNSWORTH

The exposure to the elements when eating alfresco on the seashores of Provence is at once a highlight and a hazard. Sand gliding between the toes, salty breeze kissing the skin, tumbler of ice-cold wine in hand and a *pan bagnat* sandwich in the other is the scene I want to set, so I've learnt to come armed with all the gear necessary to make sure the reality of the day is as lovely as the romantic image in my head.

The Provençal Riviera is scattered with craggy rocks jutting into the water and the welcome shade of umbrella pines, so I tend to pick the spots where these two coincide. The rocks for when the sand gets too much and the shade for when you need solace from the sun.

While weather is on our side for the most part, knowing how to handle it is key. A good cool box is the cornerstone of a Provençal beach picnic. I start with a layer of ice blocks on the base, then pile the pre-chilled drinks on top. Leaving a bottle of water or two in the freezer the night before ensures the water is ice-cold and allows you to free up some space in the cool box, too. Thermos flasks aren't just for hot and cold drinks – a wide-mouthed thermos is the ideal vessel for lots of ice for your rosé. And while purists might consider ice sacrilege in a good rosé, beach life has its own set of rules.

'A good cool box is the cornerstone of a Provençal beach picnic.'

The next layer of space is essential for the food you want chilled, like marinated goat's cheese (see page 188), *pan bagnats* (see page 191) or potato salad (see page 192). If you want to bring crudités, herbs or leaves, I pre-prep them and roll them in paper towels, then bundle them into airtight boxes or, better still, little jars. Storing dips or other bits in good-looking jars makes for a much more elegant way to serve food once you get there.

A wide basket is essential for carrying and not damaging paper bags of soft stone fruits, baguettes, tins of sardines or anchovies and saucisson, and anything else that need not be kept cold.

Don't forget to bring stylish tools and serving ware: a large hammam-style towel can double up as a picnic blanket or a tablecloth for a practical camping table. A parasol is the chicest accessory to shield you from the sun, along with wide-brimmed straw hats. Muslin cloths (cheesecloths) held in place over bowls with elastic bands are extremely useful for protecting food from flies. A selection of good enamelware is an excellent investment, as the cups will stack well into a bag and the plates are durable and look the part, too. A small stash of chopping boards as well as Opinel folding knives are also great for slicing that saucisson. I tend to bring real cutlery to avoid any throwaway ones and that makes the occasion so much nicer, too.

And, of course, since the beach is always a bit of a messy affair, make sure you have plenty of napkins and paper towels handy, as well as some plastic bags to separate rubbish.

A PICNIC BY THE BEACH

A fantastic alternative to eating out is to get organised and go for a picnic by the Mediterranean, especially if you're here outside peak season. Choose a beach where you are sure to have some space and where you can park nearby and equip yourself with a couple of parasols for shade.

I tend to go at the end of the afternoon and stay on until the evening, avoiding the hotter middle of the day and watching the beach empty around me as people return to their homes and hotels. Golden-hour waves gently rolling in, music playing, easy food and a glass of rosé in my hand never fails to make me grateful to be alive.

We often go to one of the smaller beaches, Gigaro Beach, near La Croix-Valmer, to pitch our picnic blanket, unfold our beach chairs and enjoy the moment. When bringing food to the beach, practicality is a consideration, as per Frankie's handy guide (see page 180), as well as keeping your creations relatively sand-free and cool. A spread of delicious beach-proof foods will glam up the experience and make it so much more special for everyone.

GRAPEFRUIT AND HIBISCUS ROSÉ

SERVES 6

400 ml (14 fl oz/generous
   1½ cups) dry rosé wine
300 ml (10 fl oz/1¼ cups)
   grapefruit juice (preferably
   freshly squeezed)

FOR THE HIBISCUS SYRUP
50 ml (1¾ fl oz/3½ tablespoons)
   simple syrup (homemade with
   equal parts sugar and water,
   or shop-bought)
1 heaped teaspoon dried hibiscus
   leaves

TO SERVE
ice cubes
grapefruit slices

A flavoured rosé is a nice, light way to enjoy a glass beachside. As a general observation, it's well worth using a nice enough bottle of rosé, even if it's for a cocktail, as the taste will be much better if the base is good. I always keep a few empty wine bottles with their corks or screw caps in stock, so I can easily transport a nice mixed drink for these sorts of occasions.

I usually make a bit more hibiscus syrup and refrigerate it for later use, so feel free to double the ingredients and decant what you're not using into a small jar or bottle – it will last for 2–3 weeks and is also delicious over vanilla ice cream.

First, make the hibiscus syrup. Gently heat the simple syrup in a saucepan over a medium-low heat and add the hibiscus leaves. Turn the heat down to the lowest setting and let it infuse for 10 minutes. Warning: it will be intensely coloured, so take care of your clothes or wooden surfaces! Strain through a sieve (fine mesh strainer) into a small jar and discard the hibiscus leaves.

Pour the wine into a large jug (pitcher), then add the grapefruit juice (pour through a sieve if it's very pulpy), then add the hibiscus syrup. Gently stir and taste – add more simple syrup if you prefer it sweeter, but make sure it's not too much, it's meant to be a bit tart and refreshing. Pour back into a clean, dry bottle through a funnel and seal tightly. Refrigerate and store the bottle upright if you are taking it out and about.

When you're ready to serve, put some ice cubes and a slice of grapefruit into each glass, then pour over the flavoured rosé.

BLACK OLIVE TAPENADE AND CARAMELISED WALNUT PUFF PASTRY SLICES

SERVES 6–8

2 × 320 g (11¼ oz) packets
of all-butter puff pastry

50 g (1¾ oz/½ cup) walnut
halves

1 tablespoon brown demerara
sugar

1 teaspoon herbes de Provence

100 g (3½ oz) of black olive
tapenade

1 small egg, beaten

fleur de sel

Nuts and black olive tapenade go together so well that I was inspired to create this very easy and fun pastry nibble. I use shop-bought puff pastry because it's hard to make at home and the good-quality versions you can buy are perfectly good – just make sure it's an all-butter version for a tastier result. If you are bringing this to a picnic, let it cool and then store it in an airtight container lined with paper towels.

Preheat the oven to 180°C fan (400°F). Take the pastry out of the refrigerator for 10 minutes so you can unroll it easily.

Meanwhile, crush the walnuts into small pieces (but not a powder), either in a food processor or pestle and mortar. Toast in a frying pan (skillet) over a medium heat with the sugar, a pinch of salt and the herbes de Provence. Let the nuts caramelise for 5–10 minutes, watching carefully to make sure they don't burn and turning them frequently.

Roll out one of the sheets of pastry on a baking sheet, making sure to leave the piece of parchment paper it was rolled in underneath. Using the back of a spoon, evenly distribute the tapenade over the top, erring on the side of generosity, then crumble over the walnut mix. Unroll the second sheet of puff pastry and place over the first. Using a fork, push down around the perimeter to fuse the edges together, then prick the surface a little all over so the steam can escape. Add the second sheet of pastry's parchment paper over the top, then weigh down with an empty baking sheet to stop it from rising and bubbling up too much.

Bake in the oven for 15 minutes, then remove from the oven, and remove the weight and paper. Brush the top with the beaten egg. Return to the oven for a further 10–15 minutes, or until crispy and golden.

Remove from the oven and allow to cool a little, then cut into slices. Delicious when served still slightly warm.

MARINATED GOAT'S CHEESE

4 tablespoons olive oil

1 small sliced red chilli

5 sprigs of thyme (flowering
   if possible)

4 strips of lemon zest

½ teaspoon peppercorns

2 firm and not too fresh goat's
   cheeses (such as Crottin
   de Chavignol), cut into chunks

Being the cheese of the region, goat's cheese comes in every guise here, from salty and firm to squishy and fresh, and from the local Banon AOC of the area to examples from much further afield. As one of the mildest of the French cheeses, it's particularly good for marinating with aromatics. Jar it up and leave the flavours to muddle, then grab the jar to go.

Gently warm the olive oil in a small pan over a medium-low heat with the chilli, thyme, lemon zest and peppercorns until infused but not sizzling.

Put the goat's cheeses into a shallow jar or terrine mould and spoon over the warm oil. Allow to infuse for at least 30 minutes before serving, or cover with a little more oil, store in the refrigerator and eat within 2–3 days.

MINI PAN BAGNATS
WITH FRESH TUNA

MAKES 8

4 small tuna steaks

olive oil, for cooking

8 anchovy fillets

handful of pitted black olives,
   roughly chopped

8 crunchy sourdough rolls

1 garlic clove, halved

8 crunchy Little Gem lettuce
   leaves, washed

1 sweet onion (if you don't like
   raw onion leave it out),
   thinly sliced

3 tomatoes on the vine,
   thinly sliced

4 peeled hard-boiled eggs, sliced

handful of fresh basil leaves

salt and freshly ground
   black pepper

FOR THE VINAIGRETTE

50 ml (1¾ fl oz/3½ tablespoons)
   olive oil

juice of ½ lemon

1 tablespoon red wine vinegar

½ teaspoon Dijon mustard

salt and freshly ground
   black pepper

The *pan bagnat* is the typical sandwich of the South of France. You'll find it in most *boulangeries*, in sandwich kiosks by the sea and even being distributed by dinghy if you are out sailing. It's a satisfying Niçoise salad to go, in its own round bap, and a real *casse-croûte*, which is the slang word for a quick meal. I make these luxe versions with fresh tuna, but you can of course use sustainably caught tinned tuna. Part of the fun is that the vinaigrette soaks into the chunky bread. Trust me, eating this with a salty breeze blowing in your face is just the best!

Fry the tuna steaks with a little oil in a non-stick frying pan (skillet) or griddle pan for about 4 minutes on each side, or until cooked through – as this is picnic food, it's better to cook them well. Cut them in half and set aside.

Make the vinaigrette by combining all the ingredients in a bowl and seasoning to taste. Add the olives and anchovies to the vinaigrette and mix gently.

Cut the rolls in half and rub them with the garlic clove, then add some of the vinaigrette to each half. Add the lettuce, tuna, onion, tomatoes and sliced egg. Finish with a drizzle of vinaigrette over it all, then tear up some basil and add to the sandwich. Season with salt and pepper, then close the rolls. Wrap them tightly in wax paper, tie with a little natural string, if required, to make it look cute and pack it in a cool box for your picnic.

PORTABLE POTATO SALAD WITH ANCHOVIES AND QUAIL'S EGGS

SERVES 4

750 g (1 lb 10 oz) new potatoes
(I use pomme de terre
grenailles or rattes)
4 celery stalks, sliced
10 g (½ oz) chives (and their
flowers if available), finely
chopped, plus extra to serve
60 g (2 oz/generous ⅓ cup)
fresh peas, cooked
1 tablespoon chopped capers
1 tablespoon chopped
cornichons (dill pickles)
50 g (1¾ oz) pitted black olives
16 quail's eggs
16 best-quality tinned
anchovy fillets
salt

FOR THE VINAIGRETTE

2 tablespoons extra virgin olive oil
1 tablespoon lemon juice
1 teaspoon Dijon mustard
salt and freshly ground
black pepper

FOR THE CREAMY DRESSING

70 g (2½ oz/generous ¼ cup)
crème fraîche
70 g (2½ oz/generous ¼ cup)
mayonnaise
2 teaspoons Dijon
or wholegrain mustard

The key to a great potato salad is in the double dressing. While the potatoes are still warm, toss them in the lemony vinaigrette so the flesh soaks up all the seasoning, then dress them a second time to achieve the creamy and tangy finished flavour. This is a great portable picnic salad, no knife needed, and you can take a tin of anchovies in the basket to drape over the top when serving. You can also do the same with the quail's eggs, keeping them separate and letting others do the peeling work. Just watch out for the sand.

Place the potatoes in a saucepan of cold salted water. Bring to the boil and simmer for 10–15 minutes, or until soft when tested with the tip of a sharp knife.

Mix together the ingredients for the vinaigrette in a large bowl. When the potatoes are soft, drain them and then return them to the dry pan to release some steam. Use a fork to crush them in half (the rugged edges absorb the dressing all the better) and toss them while warm in the vinaigrette.

For the creamy dressing, mix together all the ingredients in a separate bowl until well combined.

Add the celery, chives, peas, capers and cornichons to the potatoes and toss with the creamy dressing. Add the olives and stir everything together.

Bring a saucepan of water to the boil and boil the quail's eggs for 2 minutes, then cool in a bowl of ice-cold water. Peel the quail's eggs, then add to the salad along with the anchovy fillets. To finish, scatter with the chive flowers and a few extra chopped chives.

RUSTIC VEGETABLE TARTE

**SERVES 4–6 OR
10–12 AS AN APÉRITIF**

knob of salted butter

olive oil, for cooking

5 onions, thinly sliced

1 heaped teaspoon Dijon mustard

1–2 small aubergines (eggplants;
thinner ones are better
for this), sliced into 7 mm
(¼ in) rounds

4–5 tomatoes, thinly sliced

basil leaves, to serve
(or *pistou*, see page 127)

salt

FOR THE PASTRY

200 g (7 oz/1²/₃ cups) plain
(all-purpose) flour, plus extra
for dusting

½ teaspoon salt

1 teaspoon caster
(superfine) sugar

225 g (8 oz) cold salted
butter, cubed

75 ml (2½ fl oz/5 tablespoons)
ice-cold water

The rustic, savoury, free-form galette seems to have gained more popularity across the pond than it has in its actual country of origin. While the French are rather finickity with their pristine pastries – and as a result more likely to leave the expert pâtissier to it, rather than attempt them at home – the joy of the galette lies in its ease of shaping, allowing you to perfect the extra-flaky crust yourself. This makes a large tart perfect for feeding a crowd as a nibble or picnic dish.

First, make the pastry. Put the flour, salt and sugar into a large bowl and add the cubed butter. Using your fingertips, rub the butter into the flour until it is roughly distributed (don't worry about chunkier bits of butter, they add to the flakiness). Add the cold water gently, shuffling it around with your fingers but not kneading it. Tip the mixture out onto a clean and lightly floured work surface, then gently but firmly press the dough together until it forms a very rough ball. Use a floured rolling pin to roll it out to a rectangle (don't worry if it's still rough), then fold it in thirds. Roll it out the other way and repeat. Do this twice more, then roll out to a 30 × 20 cm (12 × 8 in) rectangle on a piece of baking parchment and place on a tray or cutting board in the refrigerator to chill for at least 30 minutes.

Heat the butter and a good glug of oil in a wide frying pan (skillet) over a medium heat, then once the butter is foaming, add the onions and a generous pinch of salt. Cook for 15–20 minutes, partly covered, stirring every so often. Once the onions are soft and sticky (you don't want them too coloured), remove from the pan and set aside to cool.

Preheat the oven to 180°C fan (400°F).

Remove the pastry from the refrigerator and roll it out to about 5 mm (¼ in) thick. Slightly trim the edges and fold the over a little to create a thicker edge, holding in the vegetables. Spread the mustard over the pastry leaving a 3 cm (1¼ in) border around the edge. Spread the onions out as evenly as possible on top, then layer on the aubergine and tomato slices, half overlapping. Brush lightly with oil and season with salt.

Bake in the oven for 30–40 minutes until the pastry is crisp and the vegetables are soft. Remove from the oven and allow to cool, then top with basil leaves or drizzle with *pistou*.

SLOW-ROASTED CHICKEN LOLLIPOPS WITH ESPELETTE PEPPER AND HERBS

SERVES 4

2 garlic cloves, crushed

2 tablespoons olive oil

2 tablespoons Espelette pepper
(or Aleppo or cayenne pepper)

2 teaspoons dried oregano

1 teaspoon demerara
brown sugar

12 chicken drumsticks

salt and freshly ground
black pepper

Chicken drumsticks are always a win for a picnic to be eaten by the sea or poolside, especially if they have been slow-roasted so the meat almost falls off the bone. Always buy the best chicken you can find – free-range or organic tastes so much better, so I always try to go for that. Marinating the chicken overnight gets you extra brownie points, but is not essential – but do try to leave it for a couple of hours.

Preheat the oven to 160°C fan (350°F) and line a baking tray (pan) with parchment paper.

Combine the garlic and olive oil in a small bowl. In a shallow dish, combine the Espelette pepper, oregano, sugar and some pepper and salt.

Prepare the chicken lollipops by slicing around the thin end of the drumstick to cut the tendons, then push all the meat to the top. Remove the skin around the bottom of the drumstick, if you wish. Using a small brush, cover the drumsticks in the garlic oil, then dab them into the spice mix so they are covered all over. Line them up on the prepared baking tray and roast in the oven for 1½–2 hours. You want them to be succulent and for the meat to be falling off the bone, so if they still feel firm put them back in the oven for a bit longer. If they're not crispy enough, you can turn the heat up to 180°C fan (400°F) for the last 15 minutes.

Remove from the oven, plate up and enjoy.

FAVOURITE BEACH DESTINATIONS

Beach destinations on this coastline are plentiful, but here is a little list of our personal favourites over the years. As a rule, all car parks near the beaches are paid for. Booking in season for bars or restaurants is essential, it's always busy. Many are closed over winter and well into spring, so double check online if you are planning to eat somewhere out of season.

Anse de Méjean, Toulon

Difficult to access by car, so be prepared to walk a bit along the coastal path to reach this small rocky bay, with fishermen's huts and restaurants by the water. A very romantic place to spend a few hours.

Pampelonne, Ramatuelle

A vast bay, just behind Saint-Tropez, with perfectly white sand and numerous cool beach clubs. Plenty of space for everyone!

Gigaro, La Croix-Valmer

Just next door to Pampelonne is Gigaro beach, a wide bay framed by pine forests. There are some nice beach clubs and snack bars with good parking.

Le Suveret, Théoule-sur-Mer

This is a very sweet fishing village with a small port, and the beaches are small, but in a very nice setting. Plenty of restaurants and cafés are nearby.

198

Cap Taillat, Ramatuelle

This peninsula is best accessed by boat and is a stunning place to drop anchor and swim to shore. It can also be reached on foot via the Escalet or Gigaro beaches, where there is parking (about an hour walk from each). It is a stunning nature reserve with small beaches, natural rock formations and exceptional flora and fauna. Make sure you are well equipped with good footwear, snacks and water.

L'Estagnol or Le Pellegrin, Bormes les Mimosas

The best family choices because both have parking that takes you very close to the beach. The waters are shallow at the beginning and beautifully turquoise. Some nice, fairly high-end restaurants.

Paloma, Saint-Jean-Cap-Ferrat

Tiny but stunning, with beautiful adjacent villas and a view from Eze to Cap-d'Ail. Parking is not easy in season, so be prepared to walk a bit to get there.

La Gravette and Le Ponteil, Antibes

Antibes has some larger beaches right in front of the old town. They are, of course, very busy, especially in season, but it's a very nice way to combine a day trip with some sightseeing and culture with a few moments of sitting in the sand and looking out to sea!

Promenade des Anglais, Nice

A huge pebble beach that spans all the bay of Nice and the famous Promenade des Anglais. Great when you want to suck up the city vibe of Nice, with plenty of young folk enjoying themselves and a stunning view left and right.

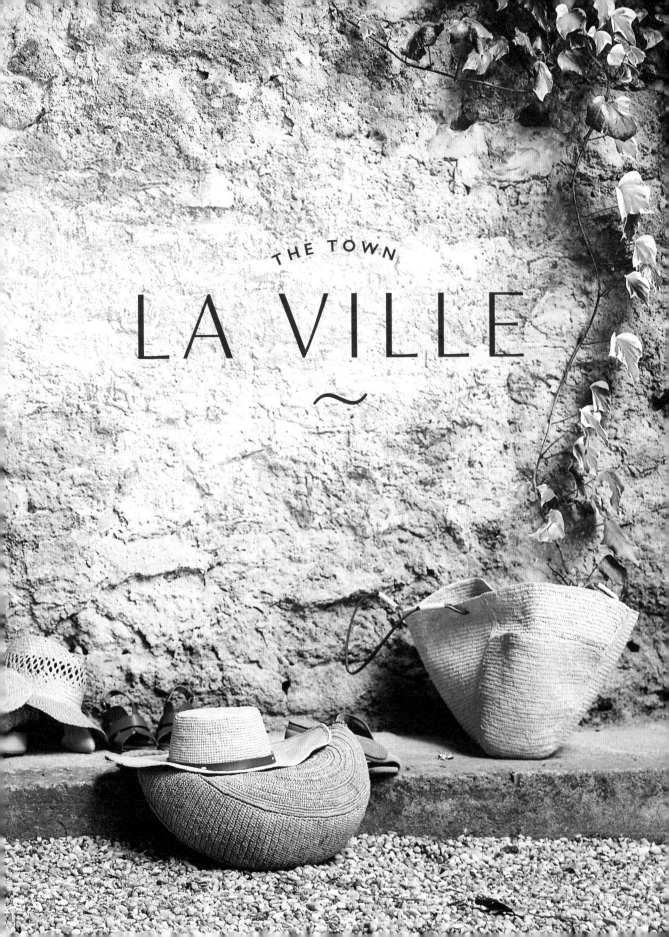

THE TOWN

LA VILLE

~

PROVENCE IN THE CITY

With all its incredible rural beauty and the glamour of its Riviera coastline, Provence also boasts some vibrant cities, like my southern-chic favourite, Aix-en-Provence. Cannes, Nice and Menton have strong Italian influences in terms of colours and local cuisine, as well as some grand architecture from the high-end tourism of the early 20th century.

Toulon and Marseille were home to the fishing industry and seafaring trade, so are built around harbours, docks and food markets. But my favourite townie destination is Aix-en-Provence, a little inland from Marseilles, which is commonly called the 21st Arrondissement of Paris. The reason for this surnom is its beautiful architecture, especially visible on the main drag of the Cours Mirabeau, with many buildings constructed with ochre-coloured stone from the Bibémus quarry.

It's funny, because initially we had planned to move to Aix (as we call it for short), and something inside me always wonders a little what life would have been like in this cool, more urban Provence. In fact, the name for our wine brand, Mirabeau, got lodged in our heads during our many visits to the town centre when we were first visiting estate agents and usually parked just by the Cours Mirabeau. I love coming here for the great shopping, as there are many independent boutiques as well as all the big brands. Most are housed in interesting old buildings, sometimes with pretty courtyards, and that makes shopping a lot more fun.

The Cours Mirabeau is not only the grandest avenue in Aix, but it also neatly divides the city in two. To the right you have various museums and galleries and to the left you have the bustling old town, shops and marketplaces. The Cours also serves as a great backdrop for the weekly antiques and flea market on Saturdays, where I have often picked up a decorative bargain.

It's also a bustling student town with a well-known university, and this lends the city a joyous atmosphere, with young people in groups sauntering down the cobbled streets to their lectures or congregating for gossip and an afternoon drink. You will see men and women of all ages sporting a look that is the perfect balance of city chic and informality, which is softly sexy and carefree. The shades of ochre and gold throughout the city lend a magic glow to the Cours in the warm sunlight of Provence. Aix is a great combination of a stylish town with a really satisfying amount of culture, set against a warren of small alleyways that are full of medieval charm, with hidden boutiques and restaurants.

STAY A WHILE

To really appreciate this city, which brings such distinct visual impressions, it's a great idea to plan an overnight stay. Head out in the early evening to soak up the atmosphere when the sun rays are softer and fan through the streets. There are many small squares and fountains, an incredible 130 in all, and it's gorgeous to just walk around and stop near one for a drink when the fancy takes you. My favourite is the Fontaine Mousse, which is just a huge rock set in a stone basin, bang in the middle of the Cours Mirabeau. It's completely covered in various mosses, and is surprisingly fed by a warm natural spring. There are also many restaurants, mostly with casual terrace-style eating, that will be just fine for an evening of people watching and letting your gaze wander over the beautiful façades.

The next morning, head over to one of the many markets or down the Rue D'Italie (one of the oldest urban streets in France), which has lovely shops full of baked goods, cheese, teas and chocolates. Aix is well known for its beautiful fruit and vegetable markets, bringing in produce from the agricultural areas around the Rhone estuary and further up towards the Vaucluse. I love popping down here to visit the Place Richelme and stock up on ripe melons and peaches. In autumn (fall), you can source wonderful mushrooms and deep green chards. There are, of course, quality butchers, bakeries and delicatessens – everything you'd expect from a bigger French city with many potential customers. Three days a week you can find a flower market on the Place de la Mairie, where all I want to do is find a café, sit down and have a chat with a friend while gazing at the blooms in buckets under the stalls' stripy umbrellas.

We can't talk about Aix without a few words on the famous *calissons d'Aix*, the local sweet speciality. It's an ancient recipe, well known since the 15th century in France, but likely based on a Roman dessert and still made in much the same way. The sweet is also served as part of the traditional 13 desserts of Christmas in Provence. It's a small, almond-shaped soft biscuit, with confit melon and orange peel, egg white and ground almonds (almond meal), which is set on rice paper and topped with a generous layer of glazed icing (frosting), perfect for a nibble with your mid-morning coffee. They are especially delicious when freshly made, so it's well worth seeking out a patisserie that's known for them (of course, there are animated discussions online about who's the best). You can buy the filling, the *crème de calisson*, in a larger pot in some of the speciality shops to spread over homemade crêpes or add to vanilla ice cream. It's sweet, but seriously delicious.

CAULIFLOWER VELOUTÉ WITH PROVENÇAL DUKKAH-CRUSTED CHEESY CROUTONS

SERVES 4

50 g (1¾ oz) salted butter

150 g (5½ oz) banana shallots, sliced

150 g (5½ oz) potatoes (Maris Piper are good), peeled and sliced

5 garlic cloves, sliced

200 g (7 oz) cauliflower, roughly chopped

1 litre (34 fl oz/4¼ cups) whole (full-fat) milk

1 vegetable stock cube

salt

FOR THE PROVENÇAL DUKKAH

3 tablespoons sesame seeds

75 g (2½ oz/generous ¾ cup) flaked (slivered) almonds

2 teaspoons fennel seeds

2 teaspoons coriander seeds

2 teaspoons thyme leaves

1 teaspoon fleur de sel

FOR THE CHEESY CROUTONS

1 baguette

extra virgin olive oil, plus extra to serve

75 g (2½ oz) firm tomme de vache or Cheddar, grated

Wild fennel and thyme grow freely and prolifically in the arid and otherwise unforgiving soil of high summer in Provence, infusing the air with their evocative dry perfume. This Provençal dukkah is the essence of these heady aromas and adds an unexpected fragrance to this velvety soup. The soup is at its best served straight after blending, when it's bubbly and light.

Heat the butter in a large saucepan over a medium heat until foaming, then add the shallots, potatoes and garlic, lower the heat and gently cook until the potatoes and shallots soften slightly, about 8–10 minutes.

Add the cauliflower and cook for a further 2 minutes, then add the milk and vegetable stock cube and bring to a low simmer. Cook for about 10 minutes until the potatoes and cauliflower are fully cooked – you want them to be soft enough that they will be very velvety when blended. Transfer to a blender and blend until very smooth. Check for seasoning and add salt as required.

For the dukkah, toast the sesame seeds in a medium-hot, dry frying pan (skillet) until golden, then remove and set aside. Toast the almonds until golden, then remove and set aside. Lastly, add the fennel and coriander seeds and toast until fragrant. Combine everything along with the thyme and fleur de sel and either crush roughly in a pestle and mortar or pulse in a small blender.

For the croutons, preheat the oven to 200°C fan (425°F) and line a baking tray (pan) with baking parchment.

Tear the baguette into bite-sized pieces and put into a bowl, then drizzle with olive oil and add 3 tablespoons of the dukkah. Toss thoroughly to coat. Spread out on the prepared baking tray and scatter over the cheese (I like to pack them tightly together, so they cluster for serving). Bake for 5–8 minutes, or until golden and bubbling.

Divide the soup between bowls and serve the croutons on top with an extra scattering of dukkah and a drizzle of oil, if you wish.

MUSSELS AND CELERY ON BRIOCHE TOAST

SERVES 4

olive oil, for cooking

2 shallots, finely chopped

2 garlic cloves, chopped

6 celery stalks, sliced into 5 cm (2 in) pieces

100 ml (3½ fl oz/scant ½ cup) dry white wine

500 g (1 lb 2 oz) mussels, scrubbed

2 tablespoons crème fraîche

4 thick slices of brioche

freshly ground black pepper

a few sprigs of parsley, to serve

Like all the classic flavours in *moules marinière*, but refined into starter (appetiser) form. The mussels and celery are piled on top of toasted brioche so that the bread soaks up all the juices.

Heat a good drizzle of oil in a heavy-based lidded saucepan, then add the shallots and cook for 6–7 minutes until slightly softened. Add the garlic and celery, cover and cook for 2 minutes until softened.

Crank up the heat and add the wine. When it comes to a simmer, add the mussels, give the pan a shake and pop the lid back on the pan. Cook the mussels for 4–5 minutes, then take the lid off and give them a stir. If they are mostly open and looking good, strain through a colander into a bowl. Return the juices to the pan and reduce for 3–4 minutes over a medium heat, or until reduced by half. Remove from the heat and stir in the crème fraîche and lots of black pepper.

While the juices are reducing, remove some of the mussels from their shells and set aside. It's a step you can skip depending on how shell-heavy you want the starter to look.

Toast the brioche until golden. Place on a plate and pile the mussels in shells and out of their shells and the celery on top. Garnish with a few parsley leaves and serve straight away.

STICKY BAKED SHALLOT AND WILD MUSHROOM QUICHE

SERVES 6–8

50 g (1¾ oz) unsalted butter,
  plus extra as needed
14 small banana shallots, peeled
  and halved lengthways
250 g (9 oz) wild mushrooms
200 ml (7 fl oz/scant 1 cup)
  double (heavy) cream
200 ml (7 fl oz/scant 1 cup)
  whole (full-fat) milk
2 medium eggs plus 3 egg yolks
200g (7 oz) Cantal or
  Cheddar, grated
8 thyme sprigs
salt and freshly ground black
  pepper
salad, to serve

FOR THE PASTRY
150 g (5½ oz) salted butter, plus
  extra for greasing
250 g (9 oz/2 cups) plain
  (all-purpose) flour, plus extra
  for dusting
60 ml (2 fl oz/¼ cup) ice-cold
  water

This deep-filled quiche is rich and luxurious, with a softly set, almost wobbly centre. While I prefer a very flaky pastry for the galette on page 195, this very easy to handle shortcrust pastry is a better choice when you want a perfectly lined tin with a deep, indulgent filling.

Start by making the pastry. Put the butter and flour into a food processor and pulse until the mixture resembles breadcrumbs. Next, add the water a tablespoon at a time, pulsing again until the dough comes together. Tip the dough onto a lightly floured surface and use your hands to press it together into a ball. Roll it out into a circle about 2–3 mm (1/8 in) thick.

Grease a 24–25 cm (9½–10 in) fluted tart tin (pan), at least 5 cm (2 in) deep, with butter, then line the tin with the pastry, pressing it into the fluted sides and leaving the pastry to hang over the edges. Prick the base and sides with a fork, then chill in the refrigerator for at least 30 minutes.

Meanwhile, heat the butter in a wide frying pan (skillet) over a low heat. Once foaming, add the shallots and cook for 20–25 minutes until caramelised and soft. Cover with a lid sporadically if the pan is drying up. Remove from the pan and set aside. Add a little more butter and cook the mushrooms for 5 minutes, or until soft and lightly coloured. Set aside.

Preheat the oven to 180°C fan (400°F). Scrunch up a piece of baking parchment and then use it to line the pastry case, then add some baking beans. Blind bake in the oven for 30–40 minutes, or until the base is lightly golden, firm and crisp. Remove from the oven and trim away the excess overhanging pastry. Set aside.

Beat the cream with the milk, eggs and egg yolks in a bowl. Season well with salt and pepper, then add the cheese.

Make sure the filling is cool before you add it to the pastry. Add the shallots and mushrooms, then pour over the cream mixture. Dot the thyme sprigs on top. Bake in the oven for 35–45 minutes, or until golden and crisp and cooked through (you need the filling to be set). Remove from the oven and leave to cool for 15 minutes before serving with salad.

ROTOLO OF SWISS CHARD, SAGE AND PINE NUTS

SERVES 4

400 g (14 oz/3¼ cups) '00' flour,
   plus extra for dusting
220 g (8 oz) eggs
1.2 kg (2 lb 11 oz) Swiss chard
olive oil, for cooking
1 onion, diced
6 garlic cloves, chopped
1 large bunch of sage,
   leaves picked; half roughly
   chopped and half left whole
100 g (3½ oz/generous ⅓ cup)
   crème fraîche
1 teaspoon lemon zest
75 g (2½ oz) unsalted butter
50 g (1¾ oz/⅓ cup) pine nuts
salt and freshly ground
   black pepper
50 g (2 oz) Parmesan, grated,
   to serve

Italian produce and cooking influences our eating habits in Provence, as we share much of the same climate and landscape of our very close neighbours. The Ligurian coastline is a few hours' drive, meaning you can pop over for a quick shopping trip at the Ventimiglia market on a Friday.

Blettes – or Swiss chard – is grown locally and is so popular it even makes its way into a sweet *tarte*, a speciality of Nice. This dish takes its inspiration from the abundance of blettes and the Ligurian *preboggion* – a mixture of wild herbs and leaves used to stuff things like pasta dishes – which is sold in big crates at the spring and summer markets over the border.

While this dish is a little on the fiddlier side, it works well to make ahead, so you can simply make the sage butter sauce when you want to serve it. Make sure the mixture isn't too wet or hot when you place it on the pasta, as the pasta will become soggy and tricky to work with.

Start by making the pasta. Place the flour in a mound on a clean surface. Hollow out the centre so it looks like a volcano, then add the eggs to the centre and use a fork to start whisking the eggs, incorporating the flour from the sides bit by bit. Keep going until the eggs and flour are coming together, then use a bench scraper to cut and scrape the flour and egg until it comes together into a ball. Start kneading until you have a smooth, elastic dough. Wrap in cling film (plastic wrap) and leave to rest for at least 30 minutes.

Meanwhile, make the filling. Wash the chard and then separate the leaves and the stalks. Finely dice the stalks, then roll up the leaves and slice into thin ribbons. Set aside.

Heat a glug of olive oil in a large saucepan over a low heat, then add the onion and the chard stalks. Season with salt and pepper and cook for about 20 minutes until very soft. Add the garlic and the chopped sage leaves and cook for a further 2–3 minutes. Transfer the mixture to a bowl and set aside.

Continued Overleaf

Add the sliced chard leaves to the pan and cover (the water left from washing the leaves should be enough to help the leaves wilt – but you might have to do this in batches if your pan doesn't fit all the leaves). Cook for 2–3 minutes, then drain in a colander and press out as much of the water as you can. Add the crème fraîche and lemon zest to the chard mixture and season well. Leave to cool.

Divide the dough into four pieces and roll out the first piece with a rolling pin to flatten it. Start to roll out the pasta through a pasta machine, starting on the widest setting until you get to the second to last setting. Dust the surface with flour. Cut the length of pasta in half vertically and lay the two pieces slightly overlapping on top of one another, to make a large rectangle. Add a quarter of the filling to the pasta, leaving a 2 cm (¾ in) margin at each end. Roll the pasta up from right to left and dust the outside lightly with flour. Repeat with the remaining dough until you have four thick sausages of filled pasta rolls. Roll each of the rolls into a piece of muslin (cheesecloth) and secure the ends, like a bonbon, with string at each end.

Bring a large pan of salted water to a simmer– a fish kettle or oval pan is ideal here. Working in batches (or altogether if your pan is big enough), cook the pasta rolls in the simmering water for 30 minutes. You can unroll one to check it's cooked, then return to the pan if it needs longer (you want to make sure the pasta in the centre of the spiral is fully cooked).

Remove and unwrap the pasta rolls. Drizzle a baking tray (pan) with olive oil and place the rolls on the tray until you are ready to eat them. You can do this up to 2 days ahead.

When you are ready to eat, gently reheat the pasta rolls in a low oven while you prepare the sauce.

Melt the butter in a frying pan (skillet) over a low heat until foaming, then add the remaining sage leaves along with the pine nuts and cook until the sage is starting to crisp up.

Slice the pasta rolls into 3 cm (1¼ in) rounds and serve on a platter or a plate, drenched in the sage and pine nut butter. Scatter over some grated Parmesan to serve.

APRICOT TARTE TATIN

SERVES 6

FOR THE PASTRY

150 g (5½ oz/scant 1¼ cups)
  T55 flour, plus extra for dusting
80 g (2¾oz) cold unsalted
  butter, cubed
70 ml (2¼ fl oz/$^{1}/_{3}$ cup)
  cold water
pinch of caster (superfine) sugar
pinch of salt

FOR THE FILLING

40 g (1½ oz) unsalted butter
60 g (2 oz/generous ¼ cup)
  caster (superfine) sugar
700 g–1 kg (1 lb 9 oz–2 lb 4 oz)
  apricots, ripe but still firm

vanilla ice cream, to serve
  (optional)

A tarte tatin is a delicious staple in most restaurants in France. When you find fresh apricots, as I often do at the beautiful market at the Place Richelme, they can be a great alternative to apples as they lend themselves very well to being caramelised in a stickily delicious way.

Prepare the pastry the day before. Put the flour and butter into a bowl and mix by hand by gently rubbing them together until the butter is absorbed. Make a well in the centre and add the water, sugar and salt. Mix until homogeneous and smooth, then bring together into a ball. Roughly flatten it and then wrap in cling film (plastic wrap). Chill in the refrigerator overnight, or for at least 8 hours.

The next day, preheat the oven to 180°C fan (400°F).

In a large saucepan, melt the butter and sugar over a medium heat until the mixture turns golden. Add the apricots and gently brown them for about 5 minutes – make sure they don't turn to mush!

Line a 26 cm (10 in) tart tin (pan) with baking parchment and arrange the apricot halves neatly on top, cut-sides down.

With a floured rolling pin and on a floured work surface, roll out the pastry to 3–4 mm (1/8 in) thick and 1 cm (½ in) larger than the size of your tin. Roll the pastry around the rolling pin to transfer it to the tart tin, then roll it out over the apricots. Tuck in the edges around the fruits. Prick several holes in the pastry with a fork. Bake for 30 minutes, or until the pastry is golden brown. When cooked, remove from the oven and allow to cool for about 5 minutes.

Now for the tricky part. Place a serving plate over the tin, then quickly invert the tin to release the tart onto the plate. You can invest in a tarte tatin dish that makes this feat much easier and is a great tool to have in your kitchen.

Serve warm on its own, or with a scoop of vanilla ice cream.

THE CITY OF ARTISTS

Artists have always gravitated to Aix-en-Provence and its surrounds. It's the city of the painter Paul Cézanne, who was born here, but Picasso also loved the area and lived for a while at the Château de Vauvenargues, which is still a family property. Cézanne said memorably after arriving in Paris: *'When I was in Aix, it seemed to me that I would be better elsewhere, but now that I am here, I miss Aix. When one is born here, damn it, nothing else means anything to you.'*

It's not far to the stunning hillsides just to the east of the city and the majestic Mont Sainte-Victoire. Cézanne painted this mountain many times, and the wave-like layers of its rocks in the pink evening light, with vineyards at its lower slopes, is one of the most incredible sights. The city's dedication to art plays out in several museums and art centres and it regularly hosts world-class exhibitions. The Musée Granet is home to classical works, but also has a great modern art collection featuring Cézanne, Picasso and Giacometti. It also frequently hosts much more contemporary artists, a recent David Hockney exhibition among them. Just down the road, the Hôtel de Caumont is an opulent city palais, fully restored to its former splendour, with an exhibition space at its core, featuring modern and more classical artists of note. On the other side of the Rotonde fountain, the Fondation Vasarely is dedicated to Victor Vasarely, the father of Op Art. There's a permanent collection with abstract and optical illusionist prints, as well as other regularly exhibiting artists.

Aix also hosts a vibrant music festival every July, which brings opera and classical concerts to the city, some in awesome open-air courtyard settings. It's a great place to come and alternate shopping, eating and art.

THE ART
OF EATING

At the Hôtel de Gallifet, in an imposing historic townhouse, Kate Davis and
Nicolas Mazet have created a fascinating art gallery, as well as a restaurant, which
hosts a different chef every season. Like us, they are also a married couple who
started again in Provence, so we felt an instant connection to each other. It's
a unique experience to sit under their huge chestnut trees inside the tranquil
courtyard, just a few blocks away from pulsating city life. As much as we adore our
country setting, it was a great pleasure to be invited there to cook together and
have lunch among friends and neighbours in this enchanted setting.

In the morning, we headed off to the markets
for seasonal ingredients and to soak up the
atmosphere of this pretty city. It's especially
satisfying to see what's arrived on the day with
so many standholders showing off their produce.

Once we got back to Gallifet, we started
setting up their wooden refectory table, which
was just perfect for a social lunch with plenty
of sharing. Kate's multicoloured handmade plates,
sourced from the nearby town of Aubagne, added
an artistic touch to this relaxed chic moment.

For celebratory settings, I love starting
with an old favourite, a garnished peach bellini
cocktail. It tastes great, especially when peaches
are in season, and to start with bubbles is always
exciting. Sitting on the sweeping steps leading
into the house, chatting with a cocktail and some
nibbles was a fun start to a lunch that inevitably
takes quite a few hours.

Once seated, a light plated starter using a
visually striking combination of produce is the
perfect way to get going. Gallifet's signature dish of
tomato consommé with strawberries, cherries and
anchovies (page 238), is a great example of how
delectable the right seasonal ingredients can be.
For mains, sharing platters can look the part if nice
crockery is used and food is styled imaginatively.
Set chilled bottles of wine on the table (skinny
ice buckets or terracotta coolers are a good
investment) so people can help themselves during
the meal, though I love going round and serving the
first glass, with a little word about the wine. Fruit
can make an elegant centrepiece and gives a vibrant
touch of colour, which can be used afterwards.
There is nothing better than a table with all the
remnants of a glorious meal and people still
chatting, chairs pushed back, napkins on the table,
all willing it to go on a little longer.

MOVING TO AIX-EN-PROVENCE TO PURSUE OUR PASSION FOR CONTEMPORARY ART

~

BY KATE DAVIES

To me, there are many distinct versions of Provence. The Alpilles mountains are wild and rugged, windswept by the mistral; the Camargue and Arles are magnetic locations at the crossroads to Provence, on the northern side of the Rhône. Further south, Aix-en-Provence and the surrounding countryside are more controlled, more genteel, despite the vast expanses of uninhabited hills that surround the Montagne Saint-Victoire. Vines and olive trees vie for space as the crags give way to the greener, rolling hills of the Luberon with its beautiful villages.

My husband's grandmother spent a large part of her married life in l'Hôtel de Gallifet (hôtel = *hôtel particulier* = townhouse mansion) before her move to the countryside near Aix, and this is where my husband spent most of his childhood holidays, away from Paris where he grew up. He vividly remembers peeking through a half-open door as a teenager and discovering a beautiful garden with four towering chestnut and linden trees, only to be told that this was the house his father had grown up in. My own father lived in Provence for thirty years, from when I was in my early teens. My first holidays in the Alpilles date back to the late 1980s, and I always spent as much time here as I could, including a job working for Provençal fabric house Souleiado before university. A twelve-year stint in Paris was a natural evolution during my thirties and early forties, and I returned to Provence for every long weekend and summer holiday.

By 2010, my husband Nicolas was organising curated exhibitions in our Parisian flat, but after entering François Arnal's atelier on the outskirts of Paris, he realised the imposing 2 x 2 m (6½ x 6½ ft) paintings would not fit, so he set out on a quest to find a more suitable place. By serendipitous coincidence, his father announced that the tenants had left the Hôtel Gallifet and that the ground floor was for sale. Nicolas immediately asked if he could use the empty space over the summer to set up a show. Stripping the place bare, repainting the cavernous rooms, setting up new lights, refurnishing entrances and offices, as well as transporting, insuring and hanging over fifty paintings and sculptures was never going to be an easy affair. But this first show attracted a large and varied public and resulted in a few sales that helped cover the costs. We will remain forever grateful to the many helping hands who unknowingly made the metamorphosis of the Hôtel Gallifet possible.

Aix now feels most like home. Gallifet exerted a huge pull, and from my first summer with Nicolas, observing the stallholders of the extraordinary markets here, I knew I had to bring their glorious produce to our garden. The table has always been my home and opening the restaurant in 2021 felt like a natural extension of the life I knew here in my twenties. Everyone we knew in the Alpilles in the 1990s was somehow linked to a restaurant, be it through the wine they made, the auberge or hotel they owned, the lamb recipe they cooked on a Sunday or the saucisson they made after a weekend out hunting.

I suppose Gallifet is a sort of homage to all of that. If I close my eyes, I see the swing seat on the terrace of the Café des Arts in St Rémy, circa 1989. I can hear the *cigales*, taste the *sirop d'orgeat*, feel the dry, dry heat on my legs and wonder at the promise of the long, hot holiday days ahead. Food featured everywhere, every hour of every day. If we weren't eating it or watching someone cook it, we were buying it or planning where to eat it next. My greatest joy now is to type the name of our suppliers on the menu and remember that I first knew some of them (the fathers, now the sons) in village restaurants thirty years ago. So goes the merry round of life in Provence.

Today, Nicolas and I live on the upper floor of the hôtel, while the remainder of the building houses the art centre, gallery and restaurant. The walls of our apartment still bear the hallmarks of 18th-century architectural embellishment. Gold leaf wall mouldings and painted trumeau mirrors share wall space with contemporary acquisitions from a number of shows in the art centre downstairs, including, of course, the vast Arnal canvases from that very first show!

NECTARINE AND THYME BELLINI

SERVES 6–8

50 g (2 oz/¼ cup) caster
  (superfine) of sugar
50 ml (2 fl oz/3½ tablespoons)
  of water
1 sprig of thyme
4 ripe nectarines
juice of ½ lemon
1 bottle of dry sparkling wine,
  preferably rosé

Summer in a glass and a great way to start a lunch party in style! Slightly more tangy and colourful, the nectarine is a nice change up to the classic Peach Bellini and works really nicely with a hint of thyme.

First make the thyme syrup. Combine the sugar and water in a saucepan and heat over a high heat until all the sugar has dissolved and the mixture is slightly thickened. Add the thyme and let it cool and infuse for 15 minutes, then remove the thyme.

Set aside half a nectarine with skin on for garnish. Peel the remaining nectarines. The easiest way to do this is to plunge them into boiling water. When the skin splits, you can remove them from the water and peel the skin off with a sharp knife. Remove the stones and put all the fruit into a mixing bowl. Using a hand-held blender, purée until very smooth, then add the lemon juice to ensure the purée does not discolour.

Pour 2 tablespoons of the thyme syrup into the nectarine purée through a sieve (fine mesh strainer) to remove any remaining leaves, and stir. Using the same sieve, pass the mix back into a jug (pitcher), using the back of a spoon to force it through to remove any coarse bits.

Carefully pour about 50 ml (2 fl oz/3½ tablespoons) of nectarine purée into a standard flute (holding 180 ml [6 fl oz/¾ cup]; if you have smaller flutes adjust the ratio). It depends on taste, but the ratio is one part purée to two parts sparkling wine. Top up with sparkling wine. Be warned, it tends to froth up, so you need a gentle pour.

Decorate with a thin slice of nectarine and serve.

CERVELLES DE CANUT

150 g (5½ oz) faiselle
    or cottage cheese
1 banana shallot, finely diced
10 g (½ oz) chives (and their
    flowers if available), thinly sliced
75 g (2½ oz) full-fat
    crème fraîche
½ small garlic clove, grated
½ teaspoon red wine vinegar
2 teaspoons good-quality extra
    virgin olive oil
salt and freshly ground
    black pepper

TO SERVE

1 bunch of radishes
slices of baguette or crostini

Its origins might be further north in the gastronomic heartland of France, Lyon, but this delicious chilled fresh cheese and herb dip couldn't be more suited to the style of eating we enjoy down south. Quick to rustle up on a hot day and with no cooking required, store it in the refrigerator to scoop up with the best crunchy veg of the season or serve with a bowl of crisps (chips) as an aperitif.

I like to make this ahead to give the flavours time to infuse – it's a good one to make in the morning for an evening aperitif accompaniment.

Faiselle is a type of fromage blanc that is set in moulds, creating a texture akin to cottage cheese when mixed. The name *cervelles de canut* translates, somewhat unappealingly, as "silk worker's brains"! But don't let that put you off!

Spoon the cheese into a sieve (fine mesh strainer) and leave to drain while you prepare the other ingredients.

Put three-quarters of the shallots and chives into a bowl with the crème fraîche and garlic. Add the drained cheese along with the vinegar and olive oil and season generously. Stir well to combine, then scatter with the remaining shallots and chives. Decorate with chive flowers, if you have them, and drizzle with a little extra oil to serve.

ROASTED YELLOW COURGETTE CARPACCIO WITH TOASTED ALMONDS AND RICOTTA

SERVES 4

50 g (1¾ oz/¹/₃ cup) raw almonds (skin on)
70 ml (2¼ fl oz/¹/₃ cup) olive oil
juice of 1 lemon
3 small yellow courgettes (zucchini), very thinly sliced lengthways (on a mandoline if possible)
1 x 250 g (9 oz) tub of ricotta
fleur de sel and freshly ground pink pepper
1 bunch of basil leaves, to garnish

I realise yellow courgettes are a bit of a luxury, but they are so beautiful, so I will indulge myself here! It's important you pick small courgettes if you can, as they are better for eating raw. If you cannot find yellow ones, don't worry, you can make this with green, or you could mix the two colours if you find both. This is a really quick starter or nice sharing dish for a pretty lunch.

First, crush the almonds, either in a food processor or in a plastic bag with a rolling pin. Put the almonds into a frying pan (skillet) over a medium-hight heat with some salt and roast them for a few minutes until crispy and a little smoky. Move them around regularly, so they don't burn.

Next, make the dressing. Mix the oil with the lemon juice and season well with salt. Set aside.

Put three-quarters of the dressing into a shallow bowl and add the courgette slices. Toss to coat well, but try not to tear them up while you are moving them about. Leave to marinate for 10 minutes.

Once marinated, plate up on individual plates (everyone should have roughly four slices of courgette on their plate). Using a small spoon, place dollops of ricotta randomly over the courgettes. Sprinkle the crushed almonds over the top. Finish with a little more dressing, fleur de sel and pink pepper. Garnish with some torn basil leaves. If you are making a sharing dish, follow the same steps on one big platter – trust me, it'll look so gorgeous.

TOMATO CONSOMMÉ, BERRIES AND ANCHOVY

SERVES 4

FOR THE CONSOMMÉ

500 g (1 lb 2oz) beef (beefsteak)
    tomatoes, quartered
100 g (3½ oz) watermelon, diced
50g (2 oz) strawberry tops
50g (2 oz) pitted cherries
4 sprigs of basil
4 sprigs of flat-leaf parsley
1 white onion, sliced
4 garlic cloves, crushed
30g fennel, sliced
20g (¾ oz) fleur de sel
40g (1½ oz) caster
    (superfine) sugar
150ml (5 fl oz/scant ²/₃ cup)
    fruit vinegar
250 ml (8½ fl oz/1 cup) water

TO SERVE

20 cherry tomatoes, halved
4 strawberries, topped
    and quartered
8 raspberries, halved
4 cherries, pitted and quartered
20 basil leaves
8 anchovies (in olive oil, ours are
    from Martigues but any good-
    quality ones will do), cut into
    small pieces
50 ml (2 fl oz/3½ tablespoons)
    extra virgin olive oil

This recipe is from Chef Josh Dalloway who created a stunning summer menu for Hôtel Gallifet. A wonderful, bright starter that makes the most of the season of red summer fruits and marries their tangy sweetness with the saltiness of the anchovies. It's a visually very pretty dish and works well as a starter, especially if plated up in attractive bowls. Any leftover consommé makes a lovely, thirst-quenching drink.

Start with the consommé; ideally prepare this the evening before or a few hours ahead. Place everything into a large container and use a wooden spoon to mix and muddle the ingredients well for 5 minutes. Set aside for 45 minutes to fully macerate.

Transfer the consommé ingredients to a blender and blitz on high speed for 2 minutes, then pour gently into a colander lined with muslin (cheesecloth) and set over a bowl. Leave in the refrigerator overnight to collect the clear tomato consommé. Check the seasoning and use within 4 days.

Serve 4 individual chilled bowls. Place the cherry tomatoes in the bowls, dot around the strawberries, raspberries and cherries. Roughly tear over the basil leaves, then finish with the anchovy pieces. Pour over 50ml (2 fl oz/3½ tablespoons) of the consommé over each bowl, then finish with a drizzle of olive oil and serve.

GALLIFET'S AJO BLANCO

SERVES 4

FOR THE SOUP
250 g (9 oz) blanched almonds
500 ml (17 fl oz/2 cups)
   filtered water
50 ml (2 fl oz/3½ tablespoons)
   cider vinegar
50ml extra virgin olive oil
1 tablespoon sea salt
1 tablespoon caster
   (superfine) sugar
2 garlic cloves, peeled

TO SERVE
2 small cucumbers, deseeded and
   cut into 3 cm (1¼ in) pieces
basil oil
pinch of sea salt
2 teaspoons cider vinegar
basil leaves

Almonds and Provence have some history. The centre of almond trading in Europe in the 19th century was in Aix and there were extensive plantations of the trees with the beautiful white flowers. It used to be a prized ingredient for nougat and, of course, for the Calisson D'Aix. There is a small renaissance in the region, especially around the Valensole area, already famous for lavender plantations, so this ajo blanco is a nice nod to this revival.

To make the soup, place everything into a blender and blitz on high speed for two minutes. Leave for 5 minutes and then repeat. Do this five times, until the mixture is very smooth. Pass through a sieve (fine mesh strainer), then chill in the refrigerator.

When cold, check the seasoning and adjust as necessary. Any leftovers can be used up within 4 days. It makes a great salad dressing, too.

To serve, dress the cucumber in a little of the basil oil, sea salt and vinegar. Pour about 100 ml (3½ fl oz/scant ½ cup) of the ajo blanco into a chilled bowl and top with six pieces of cucumber. Drizzle with a bit more basil oil, garnish with some roughly torn basil leaves and serve.

SALT-BAKED CELERIAC WITH CREAMY MUSTARD DRESSING

SERVES 4

1 large celeriac (celery root),
 lightly scrubbed
1 tablespoon olive oil
2 tablespoons salt,
 plus extra for baking
1–2 pears or apples, thinly sliced
 and rubbed with lemon juice
50 g (1¾ oz) Roquefort,
 crumbled
40 g (1¼ oz/¼ cup) blanched
 hazelnuts, toasted
handful of rocket (arugula)
 or watercress leaves
extra virgin olive oil, for drizzling

FOR THE DRESSING
100 g (3½ oz) crème fraîche
1 tablespoon wholegrain mustard
juice of ½ lemon,
 plus extra as needed
salt and freshly ground
 black pepper

This is a lighter riff on the perennial bistro fixture, celeriac (celery root) remoulade. It works well as an easy but elegant sharing dish or individually plated as a starter. It's also lovely as a side to roast chicken or steak.

Preheat the oven to 170°C fan (375°F).

Rub the celeriac with the olive oil and 2 tablespoons of salt. Scatter a layer of salt in the base of a casserole dish (Dutch oven) and place the celeriac on it. Cover and bake in the oven for 2 hours, then uncover and bake for a further 45 minutes, or until golden. You want it to be soft to the point of a knife all the way through, but the flesh should still be firm enough to slice.

When the celeriac is ready, make the dressing. Mix together the crème fraîche, mustard and lemon juice in a bowl with plenty of salt and black pepper.

Thinly slice the celeriac into ribbons and assemble with the pears or apples. Drizzle with the dressing, scatter with the crumbled cheese, nuts and the salad leaves. Add some extra olive oil and serve.

SEVEN-HOUR LAMB SHOULDER ON A BED OF HERBS AND COCO BEANS

SERVES 4–6

olive oil, for cooking

1 bone-in shoulder of lamb

1 bulb of garlic, cut through
the centre

4 red onions, halved

handful of rosemary and
thyme sprigs

350–500 ml (12–17 fl oz/
1½–generous 2 cups)
chicken stock

240 g (8½ oz) podded coco
(borlotti) beans (or soaked
dried beans)

500 g (1 lb 2 oz) cherry
tomatoes on the vine

salt and freshly ground
black pepper

Historically, a seven-hour lamb would be cooked in the low residual heat of a wood-fired oven as it cooled off, and I can attest to this method working beautifully and efficiently. But failing that luxury, the oven will do the job. Coco beans (also known as borlotti or cranberry beans) arrive dressed in little pink speckled pods in early summer and podding them is a favourite mindful activity for those who enjoy such pursuits. If using dried beans, soak them in cold water for half a day before cooking, to help them along.

Preheat the oven to 130°C fan (300°F).

Heat a good glug of oil in a large heavy-based casserole dish (Dutch oven) over a medium heat, then season the lamb all over and add to the pan, skin-side down. Move the lamb around every 4–5 minutes until it is browned all over. Remove and set aside.

Add another glug of oil to the pan, then add the garlic halves, cut-sides down. Add the onions and herbs. Let them cook for 2–3 minutes until they start to colour, then add the stock. Bring to the boil, then return the lamb shoulder to the pan, skin-side up. Place a lid on top or grease a piece of foil and cover the lamb before transferring to the oven to cook for 5–7 hours. For the last 2 hours of the lamb cooking, add the beans and more stock, if you find the liquid has dried up.

Put the tomatoes into a small baking dish and drizzle with oil and season. Place in the oven for the last 30 minutes of cooking until soft and the skins are crinkled.

The lamb is ready when the meat easily comes away from the bone. Serve with the roasted tomatoes.

NOUGAT SEMIFREDDO WITH A BOWL OF ICED CHERRIES

SERVES 8

3 medium eggs plus 2 egg yolks

½ vanilla pod (bean), seeds
  scraped out

150 g (5½ oz/²⁄₃ cup) caster
  (superfine) sugar

50 g (1¾ oz) clear honey

300 ml (10 fl oz/1¼ cups) double
  (heavy) cream

200 g (7 oz/generous ¾ cup)
  fromage blanc or plain yoghurt

50 g (1¾ oz) meringue
  (shop-bought is fine), crumbled

75 g (2¾ oz) blanched almonds,
  whole

100 g (3½ oz) candied orange
  peel, chopped

splash of orange blossom water

500 g (1 lb 2 oz) cherries, or as
  many as you like, on ice,
  to serve

Nougat is one of the quintessential confectioneries of the region, and the flavours and textures inspired this creamy, cold semifreddo, which is studded with all the jewels found in a chunk of nougat. When cherry season is in full swing, there's nothing better than a bowl of cherries crisped on ice, which I love to serve alongside a slice of this great make-ahead dessert.

Combine the eggs, egg yolks, vanilla seeds and sugar in a large heatproof bowl. Place the bowl over a saucepan of simmering water, ensuring it does not touch the water, and whisk continuously for 6–8 minutes, ideally with an electric whisk, until the mixture becomes thick and pale. When your whisk leaves a ribbon trail on the surface of the mixture when you lift it up, you are ready. Remove from the heat and allow to cool slightly.

Whip the cream in a bowl until stiff peaks form. Lightly fold the cream through the cooled egg mixture, one spoonful at a time, until well combined, then stir through the fromage blanc or yoghurt. Finally, lightly fold through the meringue, almonds, candied orange peel and orange blossom water.

Line a 900 g (2 lb) loaf tin (pan) with cling film (plastic wrap), leaving approximately 7 cm (3 in) of overhang on both long sides. Pour the mixture into the base of the loaf tin. Fold over the overhanging cling film to cover the surface and freeze for 6 hours, or overnight.

When ready to serve, remove the semifreddo from the freezer and peel away the cling film from the surface of the underside of the loaf. Turn out onto a serving plate and peel away the remaining cling film. Serve in thick slices with an enormous bowl of iced cherries.

MERCI

As alluded to in my introduction I have been dreaming of writing this book for a long time and Frankie's arrival in the village spurred me into action. I have really appreciated her experience and encouragement, as well as her contacts in the publishing industry to help us pitch our first ideas. It has been a joy to develop our recipes together and, of course, obsess over the styling in all these fabulous locations. Between us, we had a bevy of gorgeous objects and ceramics and it's been fun to use as much as possible from our respective overflowing cabinets.

Huge gratitude to the team from Quadrille, Isabel Gonzalez-Prendergast for picking up my dream project and my patient editor Chelsea Edwards for shepherding a first-timer through the publishing process.

Lizzie Mason, our photographer, has given her all on these intense shoot days, and her energy is so clearly visible in her photography. She took all our requests with amazing grace and brought a genuine excitement and love for the landscapes and food in Provence, which made all the difference. Dave Brown, a very talented designer, put it all together in a way that takes the reader on such an immersive visual journey. The lovely Georgia Rudd, cooked up a storm on our shoot days and re-tested our recipes, thank you for your calm efficiency and making the tastiest post-work lunch and dinners imaginable. My long-time creative soulmate Sophie Bellard has been my companion on this project, and we've included some of our favourite recipes that we come back to again and again.

My thanks to my Mirabeau work family for giving me the time and space to spend on this project, as well as a ready supply of rosé to fill our many glasses. And to the lovely Domaine team, Anja, Simon and Pascal, for your efforts in making it all look great, modelling and endlessly carrying things around!

Our local fashion queen, Anne Classen from Escapade in Cotignac loaned us some great pieces for our shoots, so we could really inject extra visual interest into each chapter.

I am so glad to have had the chance to feature Kathy and Peter Bullen, our fellow Cotignac residents and authors of the Brocante essay, and whose house never ceases to inspire with all their pre-loved treasures.

The unique Isabelle from Nina Bohème showed us her lovely countryside home and baked us the most wonderful cake – I am happy to have been able to share it with you.

Merci to Graham and Wendy Porter, the owners of Lou Calen in Cotignac, for our long friendship and for opening your wonderful pétanque court for our shoot.

It has been a joy shooting at the beautiful Gallifet Art Centre and to be able to feature the Mazets' experience of life in Provence. The Hotel Lily of the Valley is a great destination, and we've had some of our best coastal moments there over the last few years. It was a pleasure to work with their professional team, Phillipine Leclercq and executive chef Vincent Maillard to feature two of their recipes.

My gratitude also to Calma House, who sent me some nice things from their collection to use in the pictures.

Now to the most important people in my life – my husband Stephen and our children Josie, Felix and George. Thank you for encouraging me to write this book and for the years I got to spend with you at home in Provence as a family – they are without a doubt the best of my life. I know you kids carry Provence in your hearts forever, even if you have left to pursue your own adventures. To my parents, Thomas and Netti, without whose unwavering love and all-round support none of this would have been possible. And for bringing me to the South of France as a child, where we spent the happiest of days with my siblings and a tiny seed of love for this countryside was planted inside me.

With love and gratitude to the amazing people I have met over the years and who have instilled the art of hosting in my heart.

Jeany
x

INDEX

Quadrille, Penguin Random House UK, One Embassy Gardens, 8 Viaduct Gardens, London SW11 7BW

Quadrille Publishing Limited is part of the Penguin Random House group of companies whose addresses can be found at global.penguinrandomhouse.com

Published by Quadrille in 2025

www.penguin.co.uk

A CIP catalogue record for this book is available from the British Library

ISBN 978-1-78488-731-5

10 9 8 7 6 5 4 3 2 1

Publishing Director: Kajal Mistry
Acting Publishing Director: Judith Hannam
Commissioning Editor: Isabel Gonzalez-Prendergast
Managing Editor: Chelsea Edwards
Copy Editor: Lucy Kingett
Proofreader: Emily Preece-Morrison
Indexer: Helen Snaith
Designer: Dave Brown
Photographers: Lizzie Mayson and Sophie Bellard for pages 86–87, 120, 125 and 175
Food and Props Stylist: Frankie Unsworth

Food Stylist Assistant: Georgia Rudd
Production Manager: Sabeena Atchia

Colour reproduction by p2d

Printed in China by C&C Offset Printing Co., Ltd.

The authorised representative in the EEA is Penguin Random House Ireland, Morrison Chambers, 32 Nassau Street, Dublin D02 YH68.

Penguin Random House is committed to a sustainable future for our business, our readers and our planet. This book is made from Forest Stewardship Council ® certified paper.